Project Birdhaus

About this book:

This is a collection of my Inktober 2017 drawings.
If you're not familiar, Inktober is a drawing challenge created by Mr. Jake Parker. The challenge is to create an ink drawing for each day of October. Because of deadlines and busy schedules, this is the first year that I've been able to participate.

To add to the challenge, I decided to do a different birdhouse for each day. Choosing this topic also forced me to work on my long straight lines and foliage. Coming from a color background, I wanted to add color for this collection of the images.
You can still see the original ink drawings in the back of this book.

Thanks for your support.

-Nathan Lumm

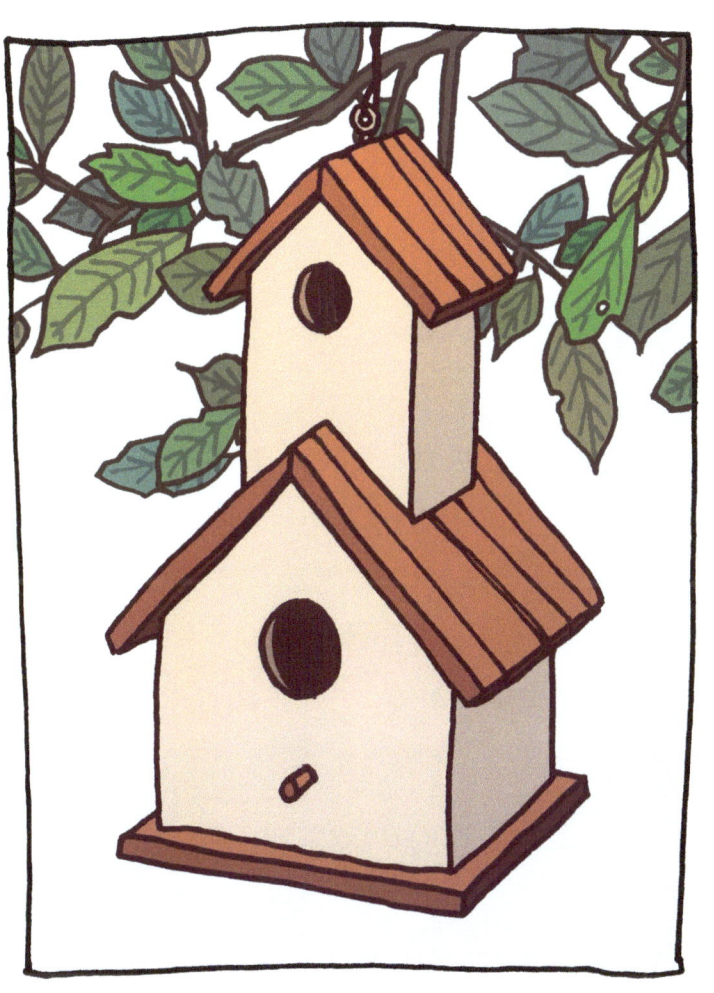

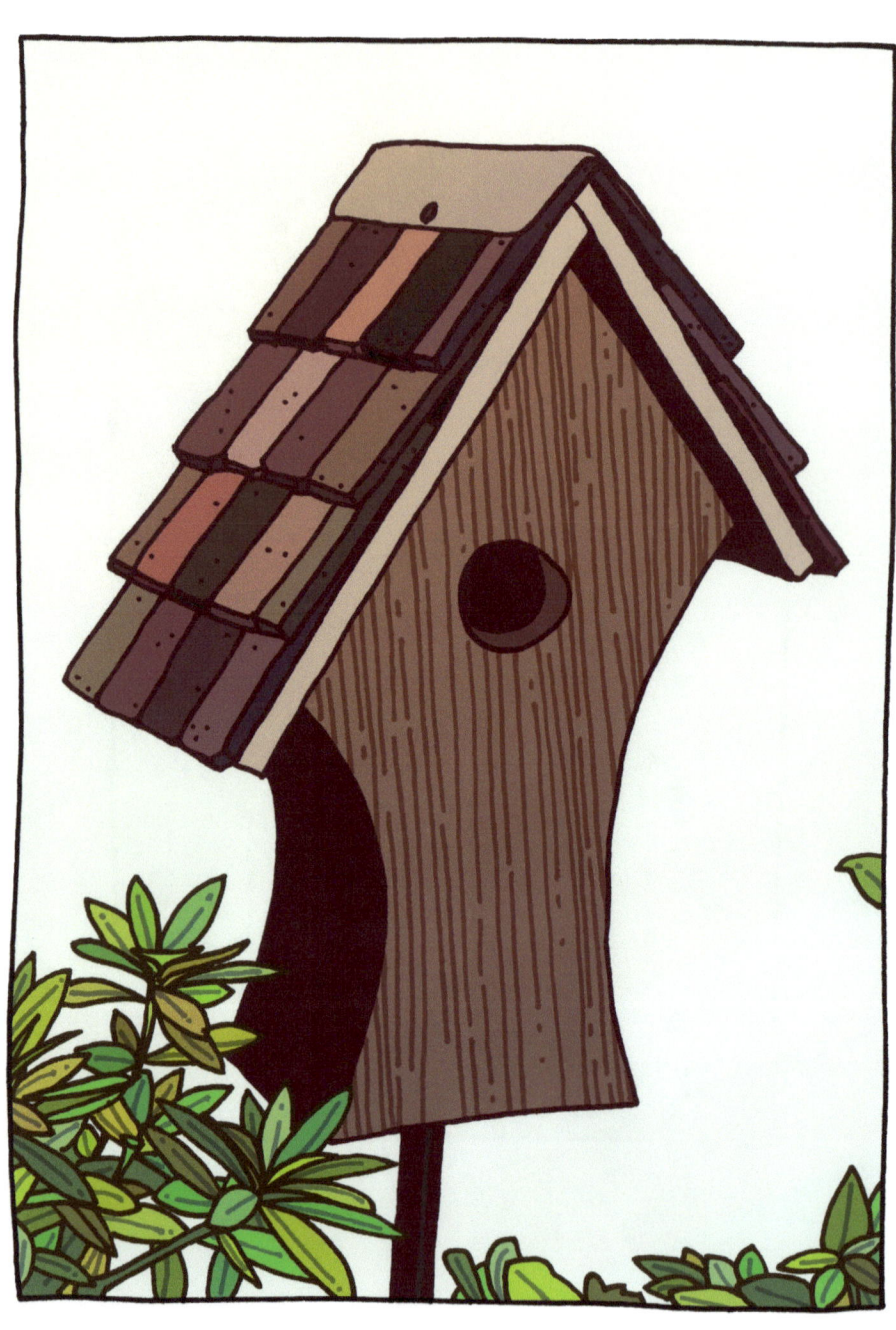

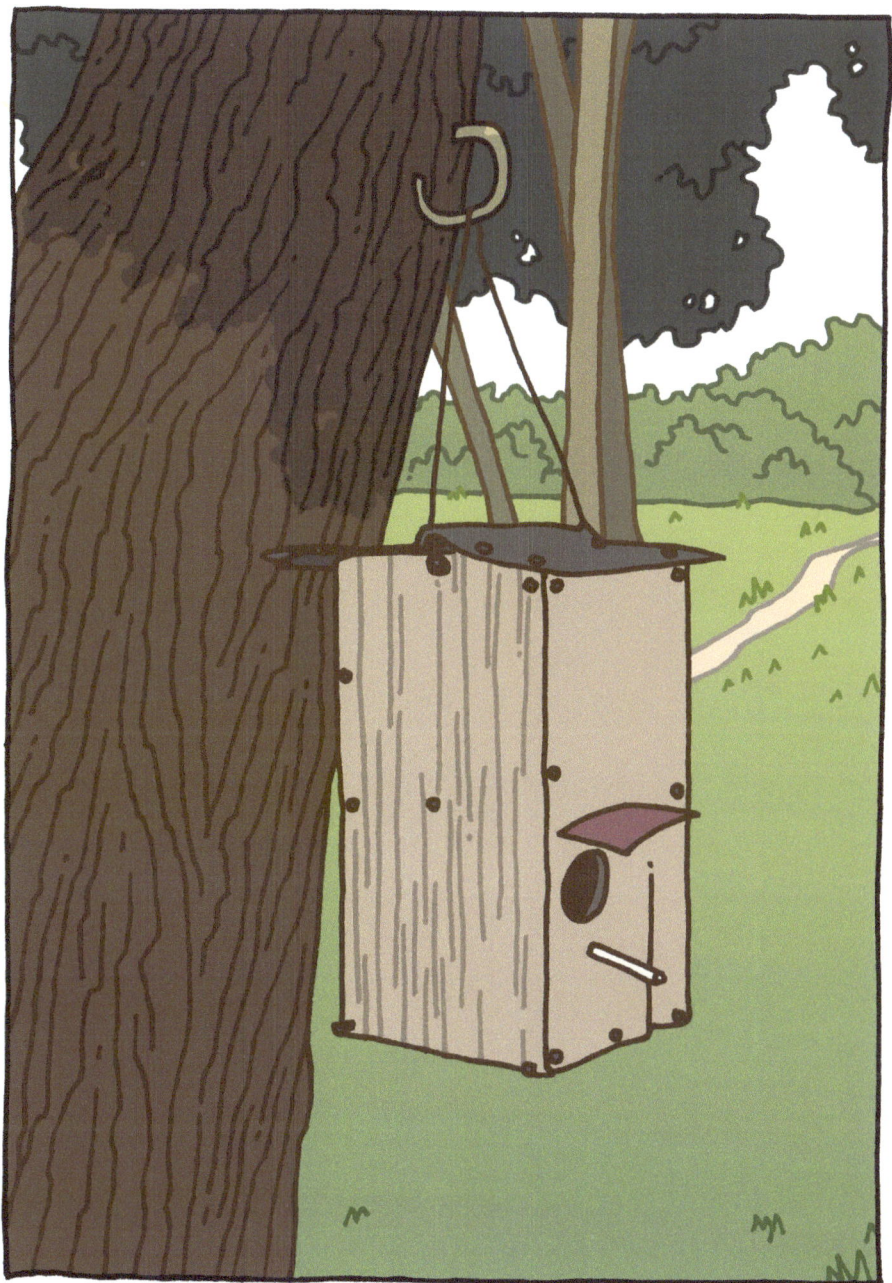

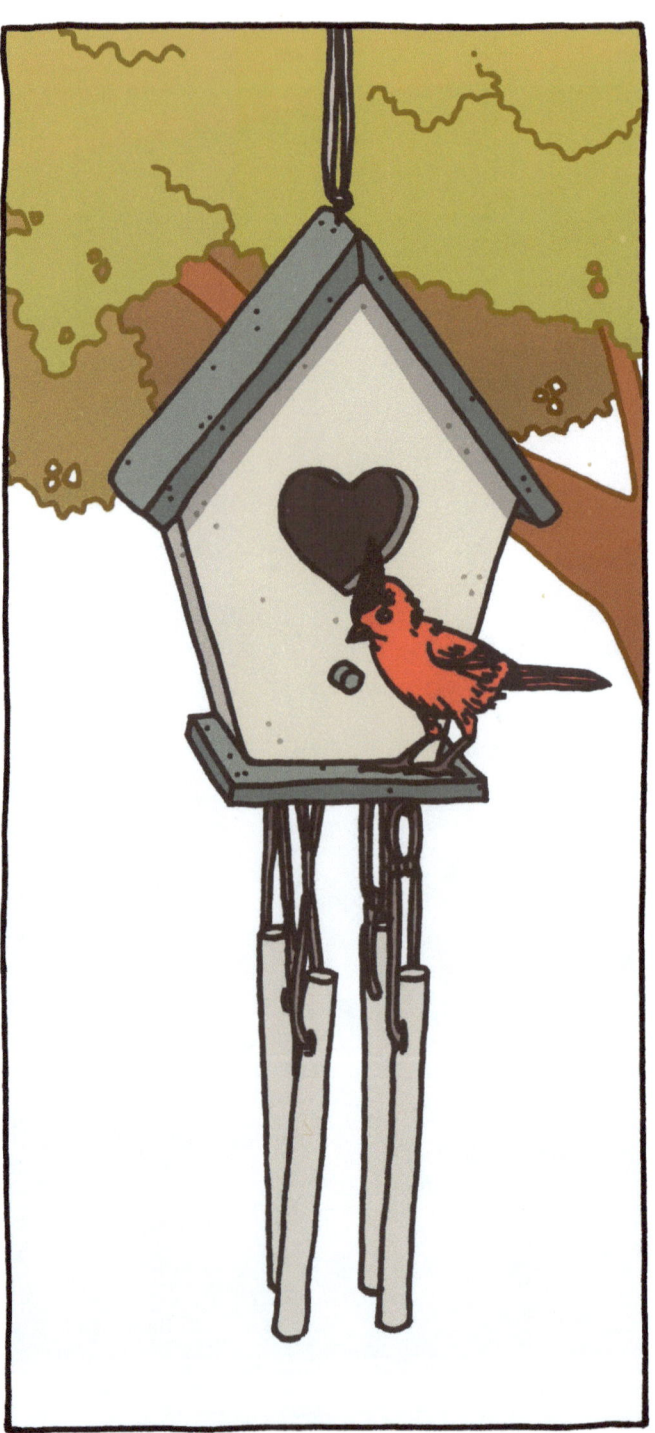

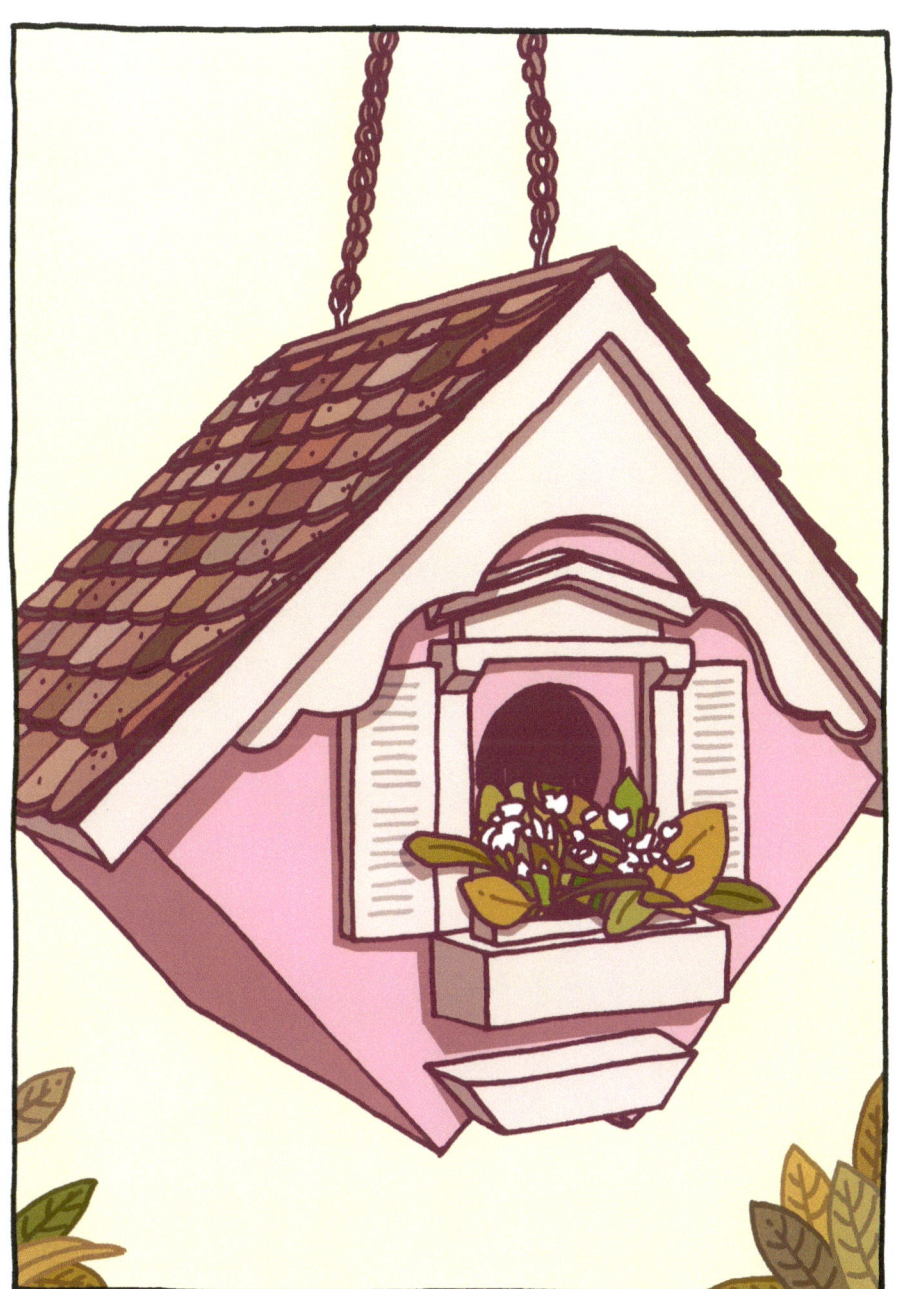

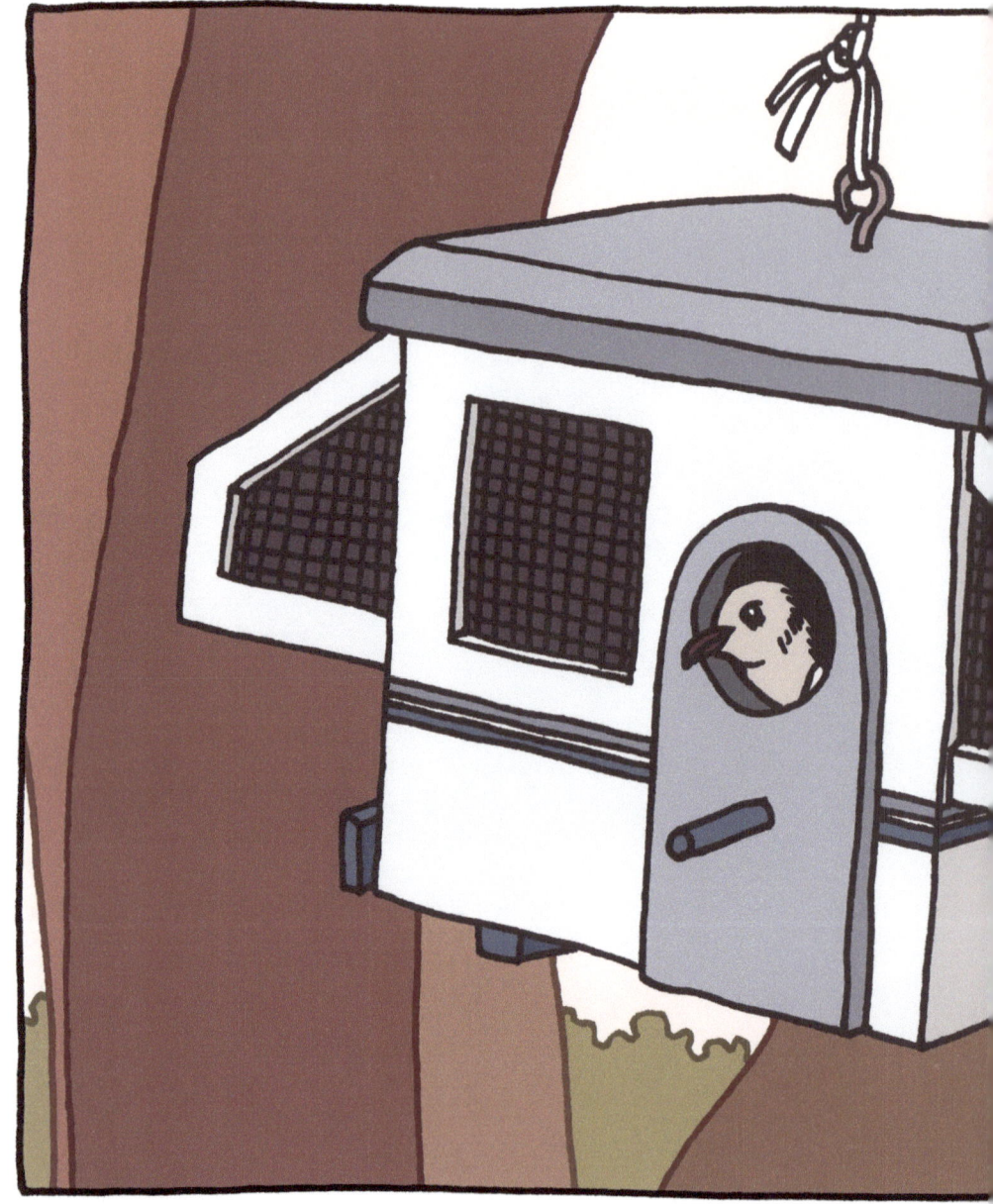

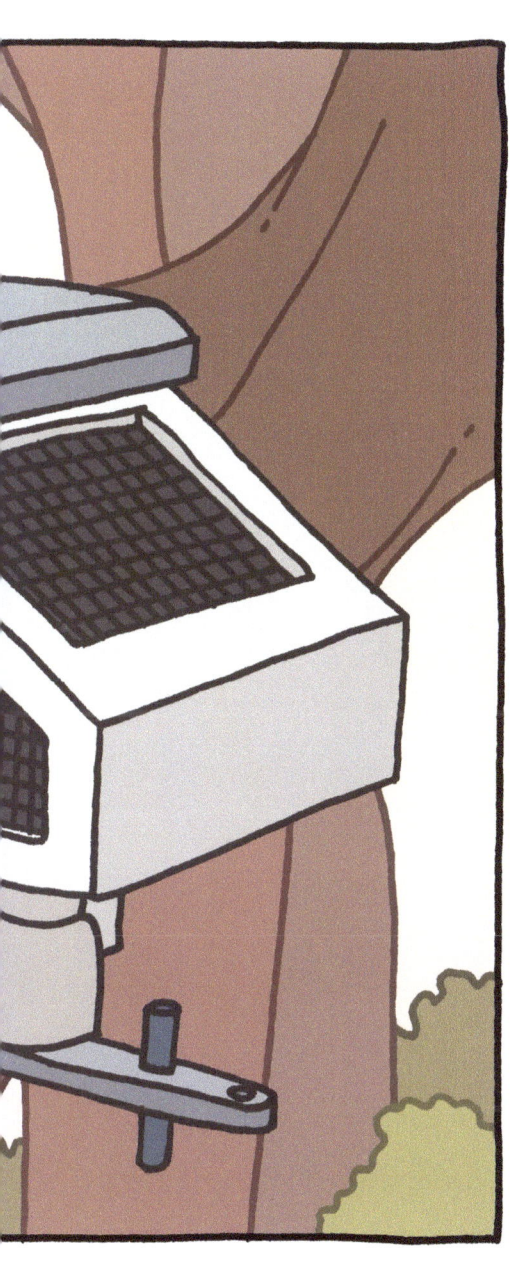

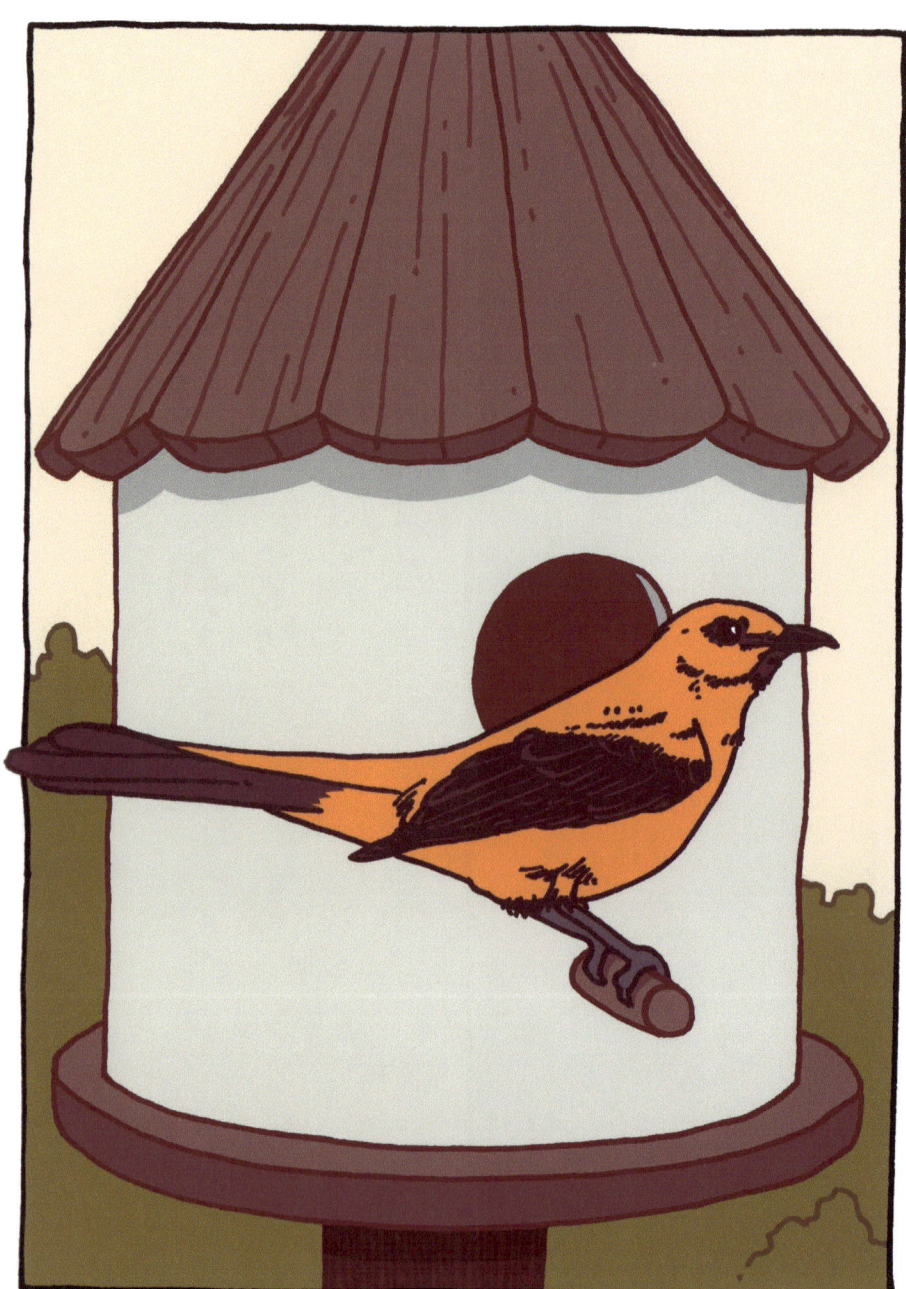

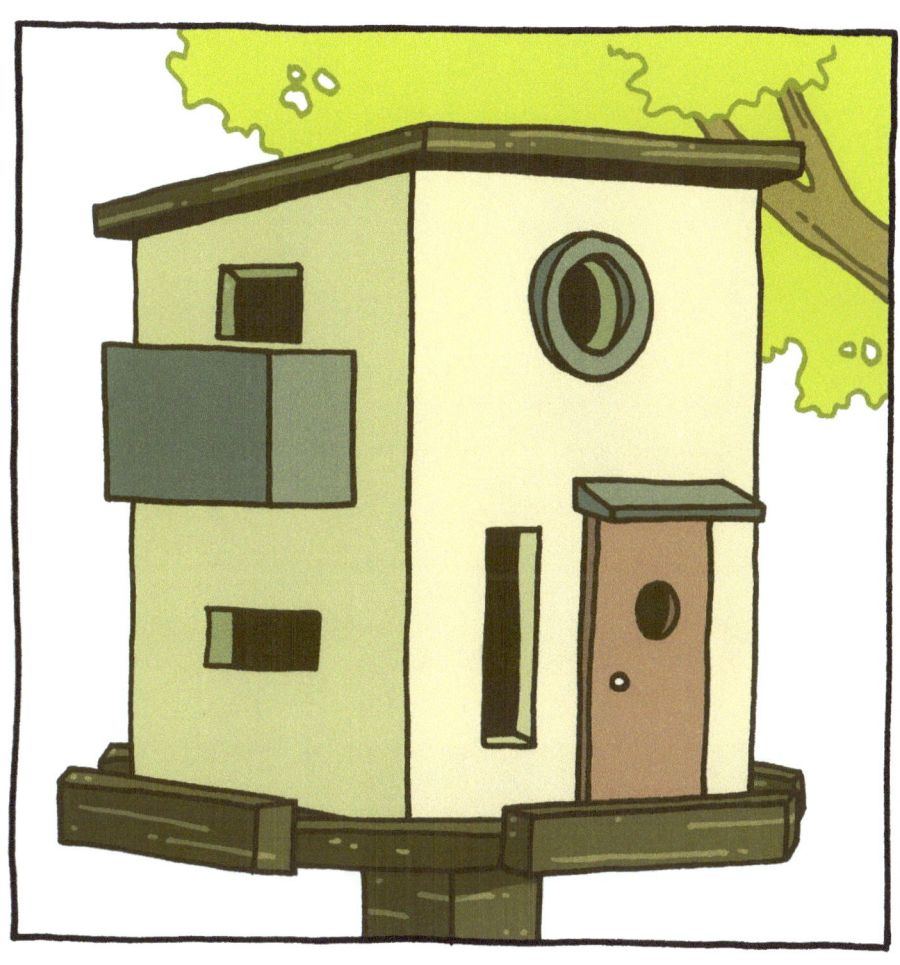

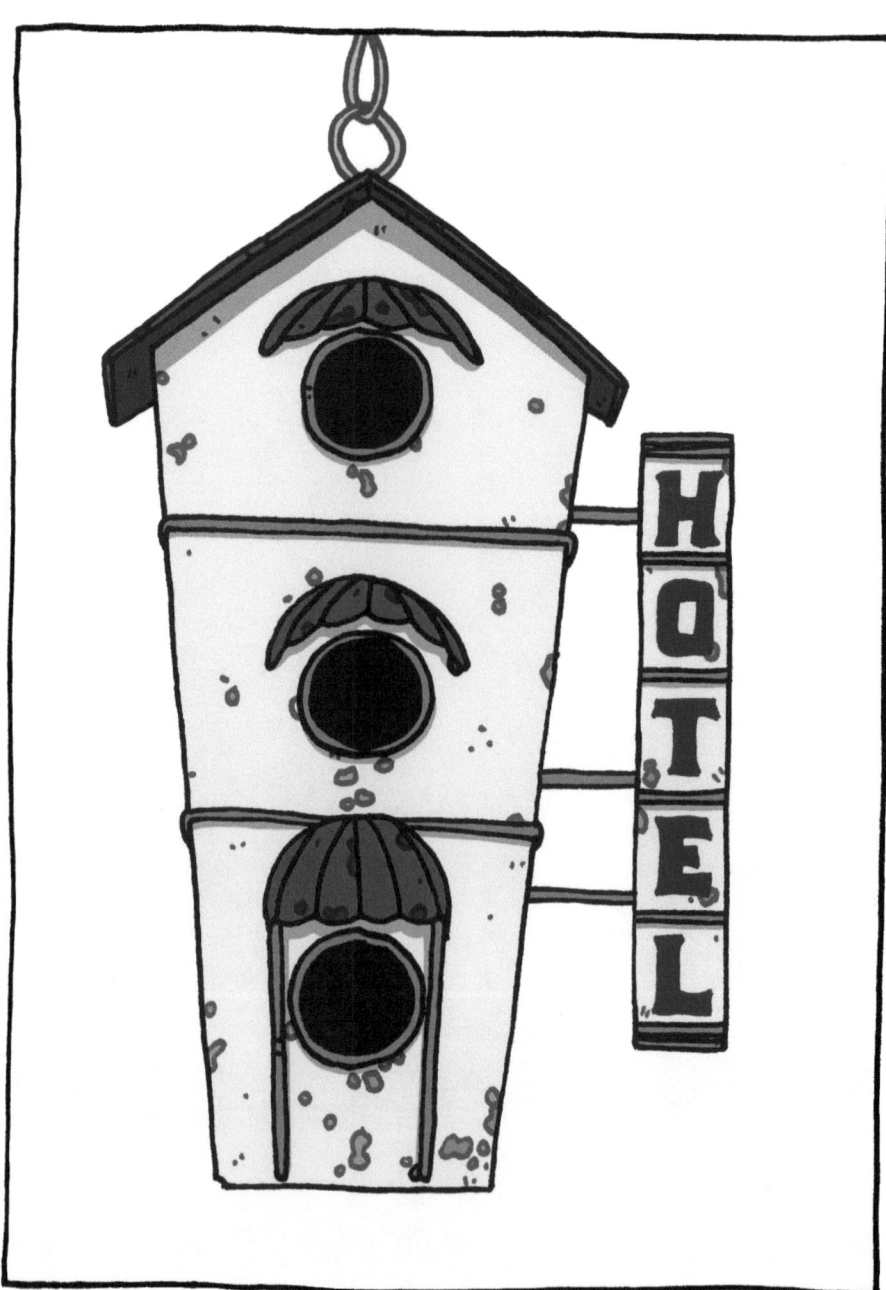

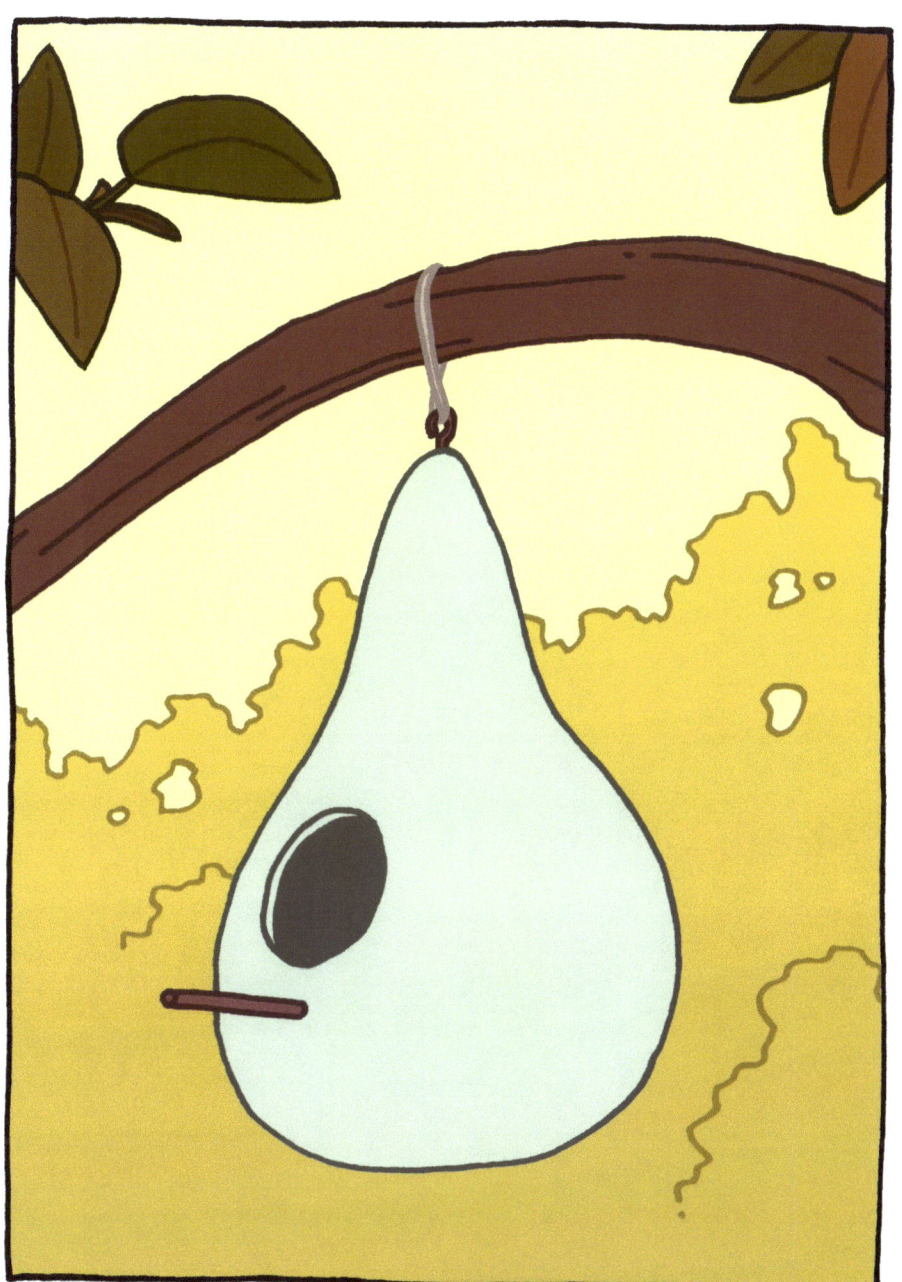

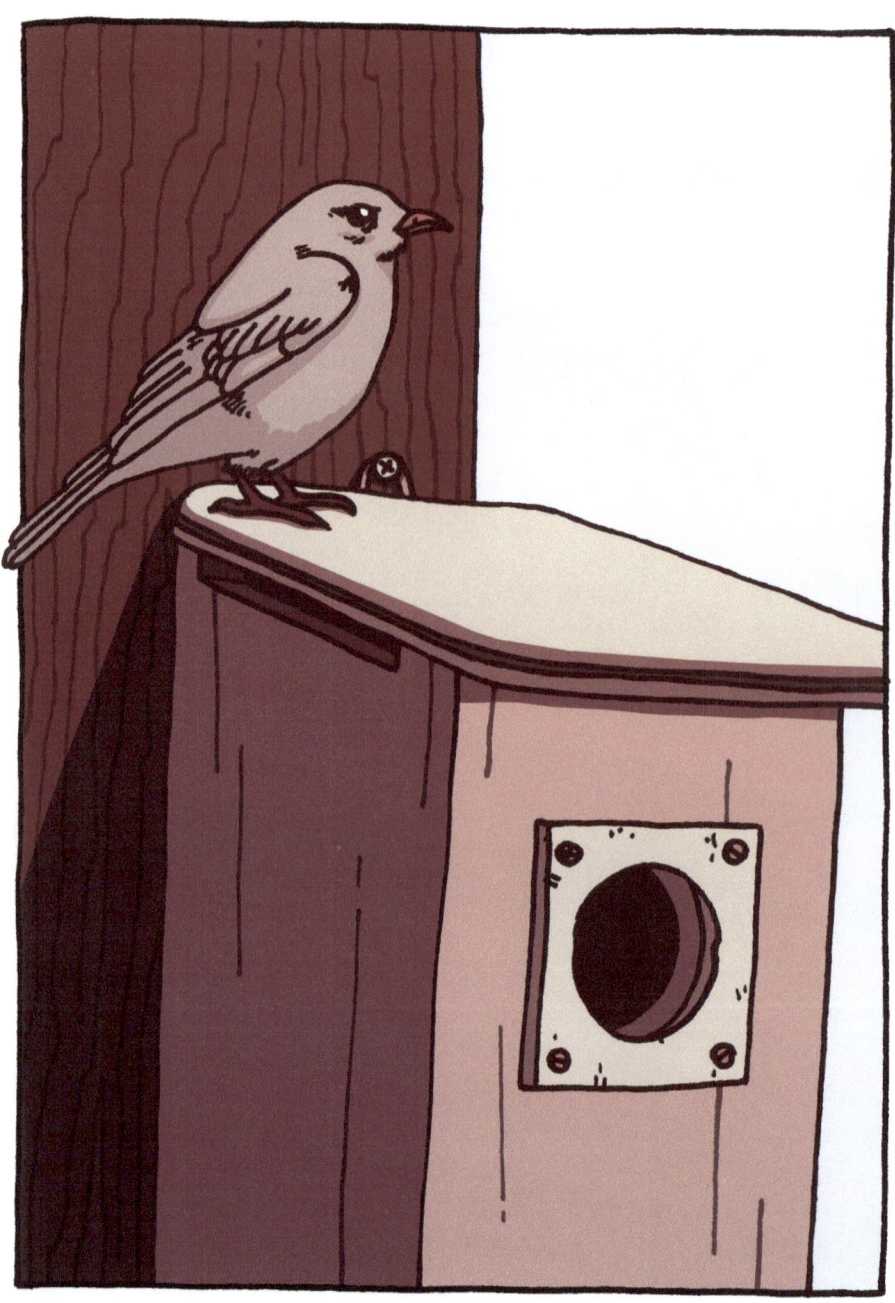

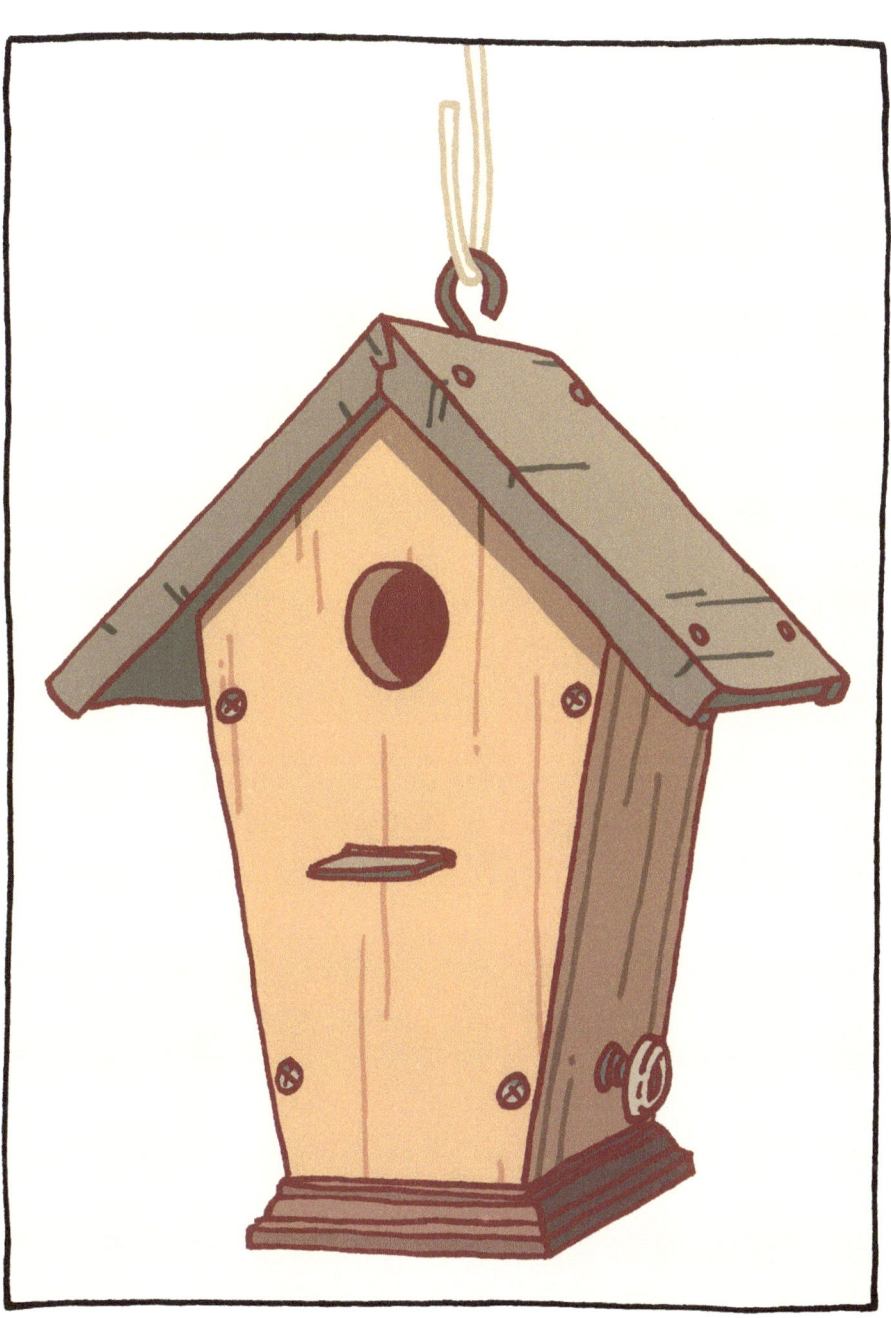

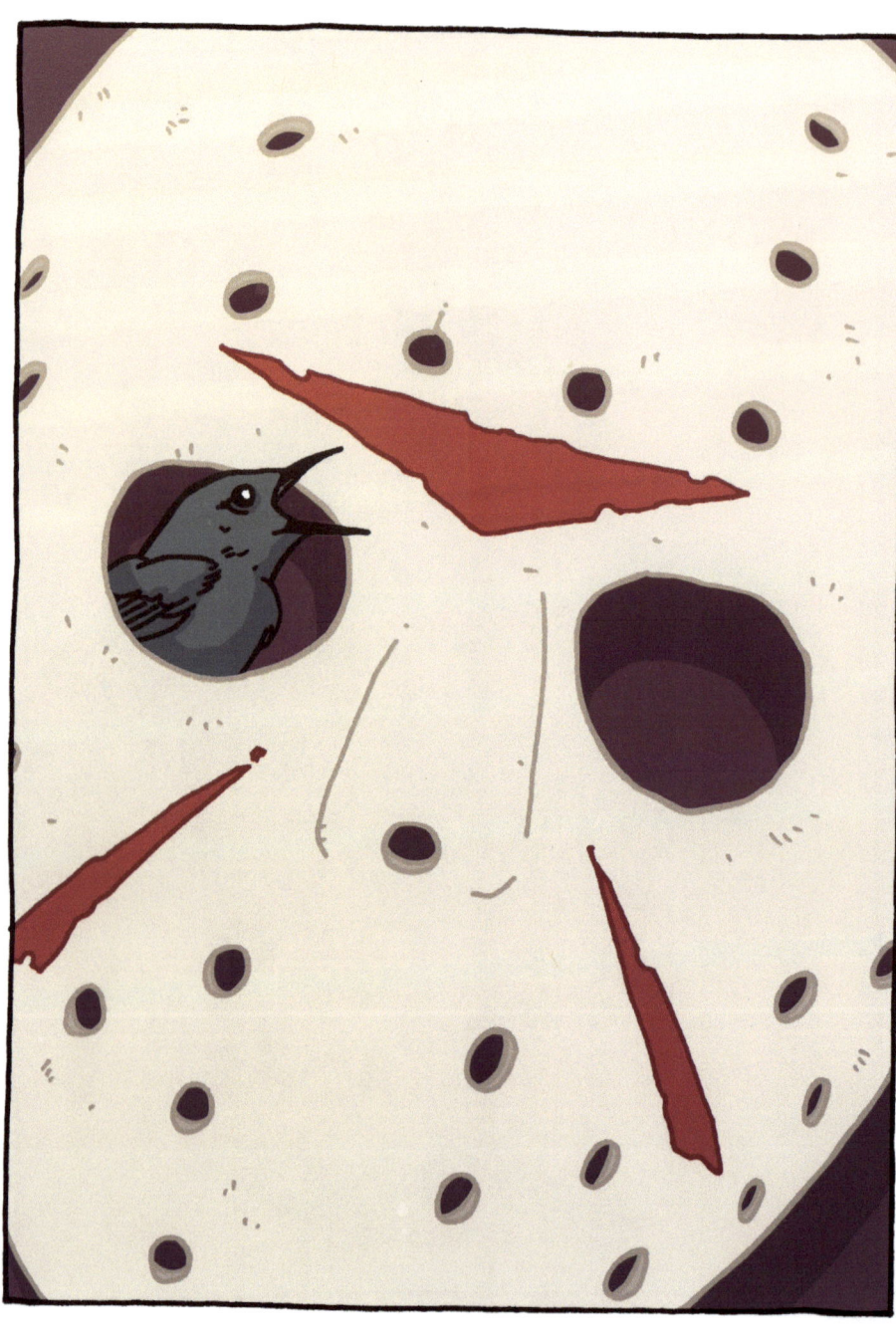

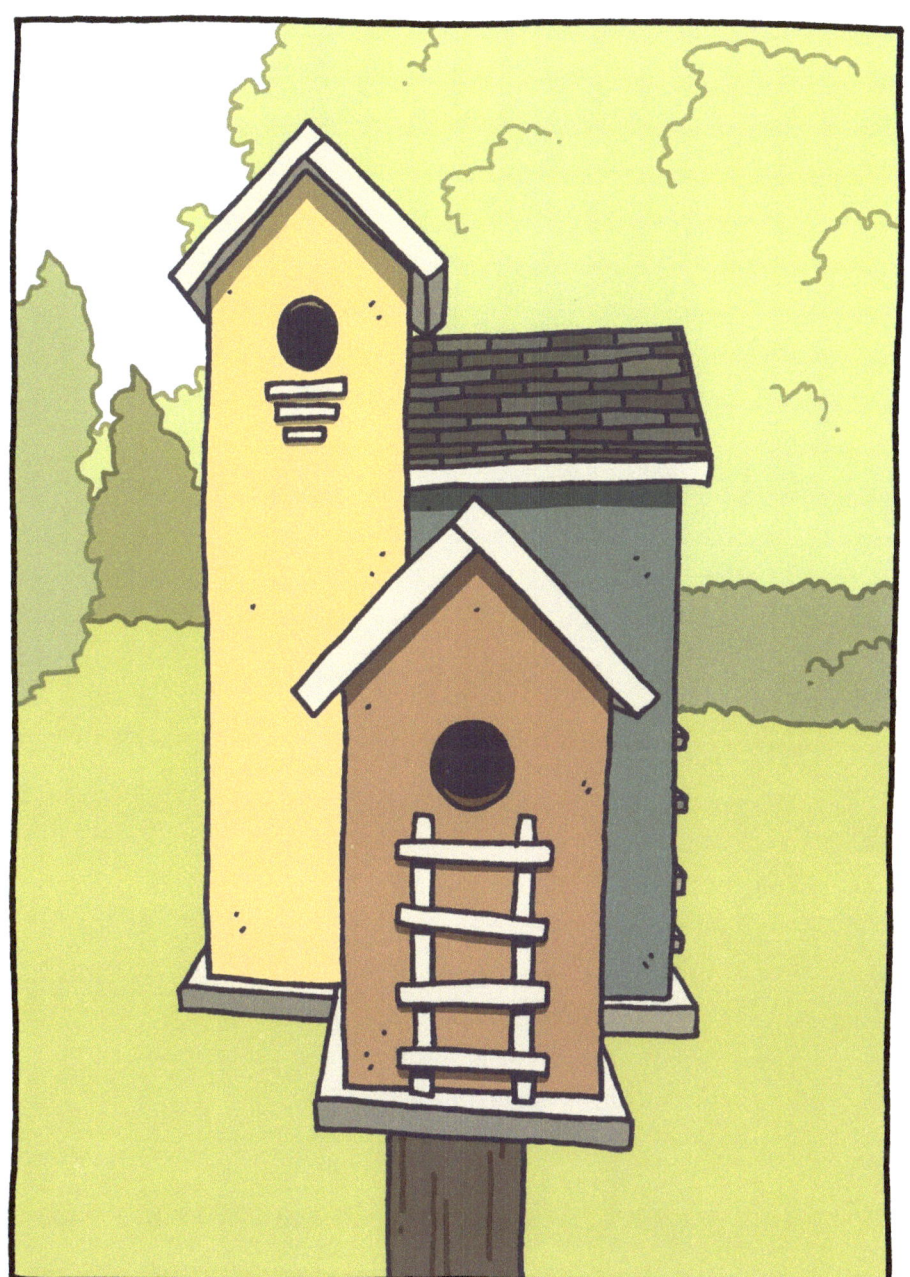

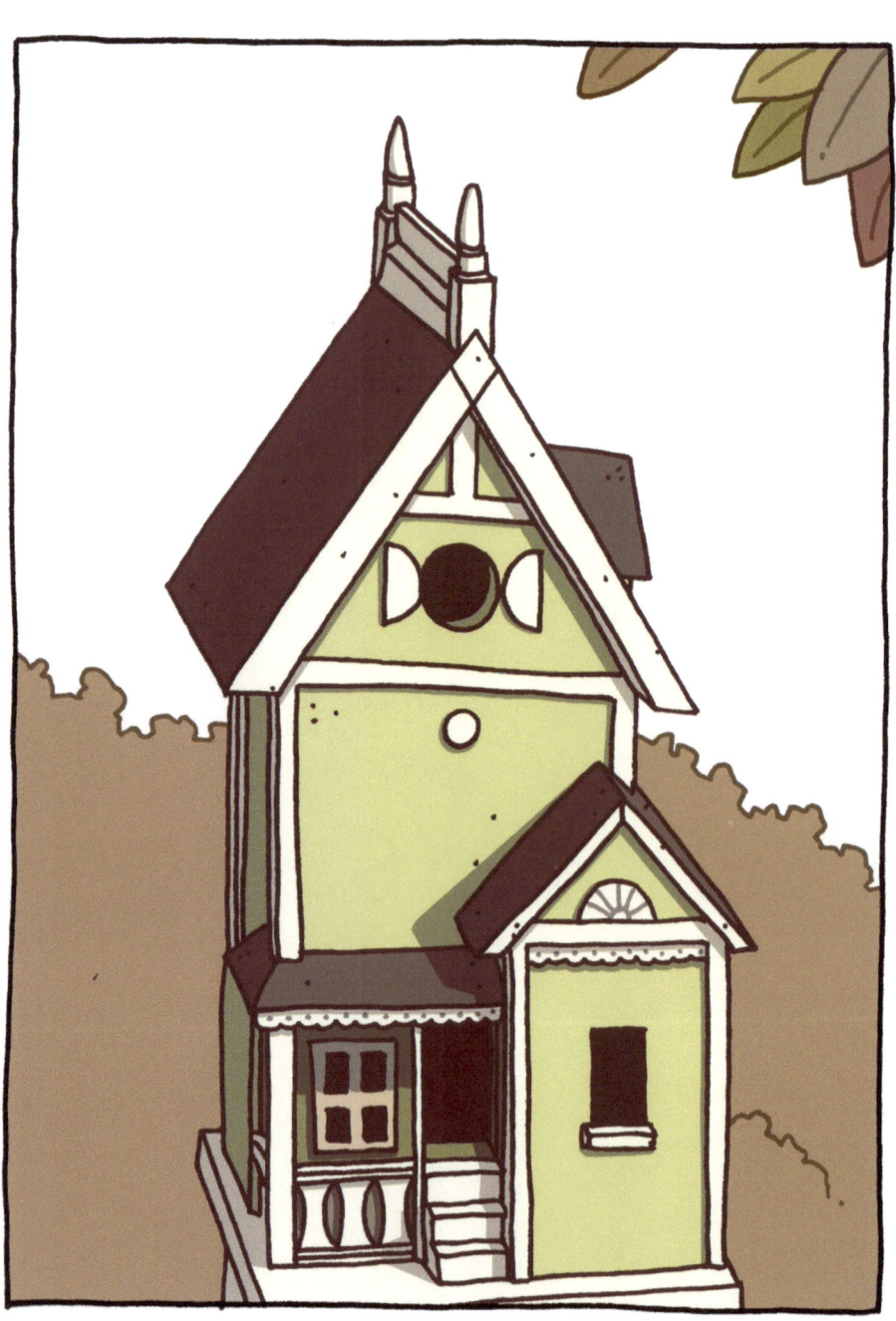

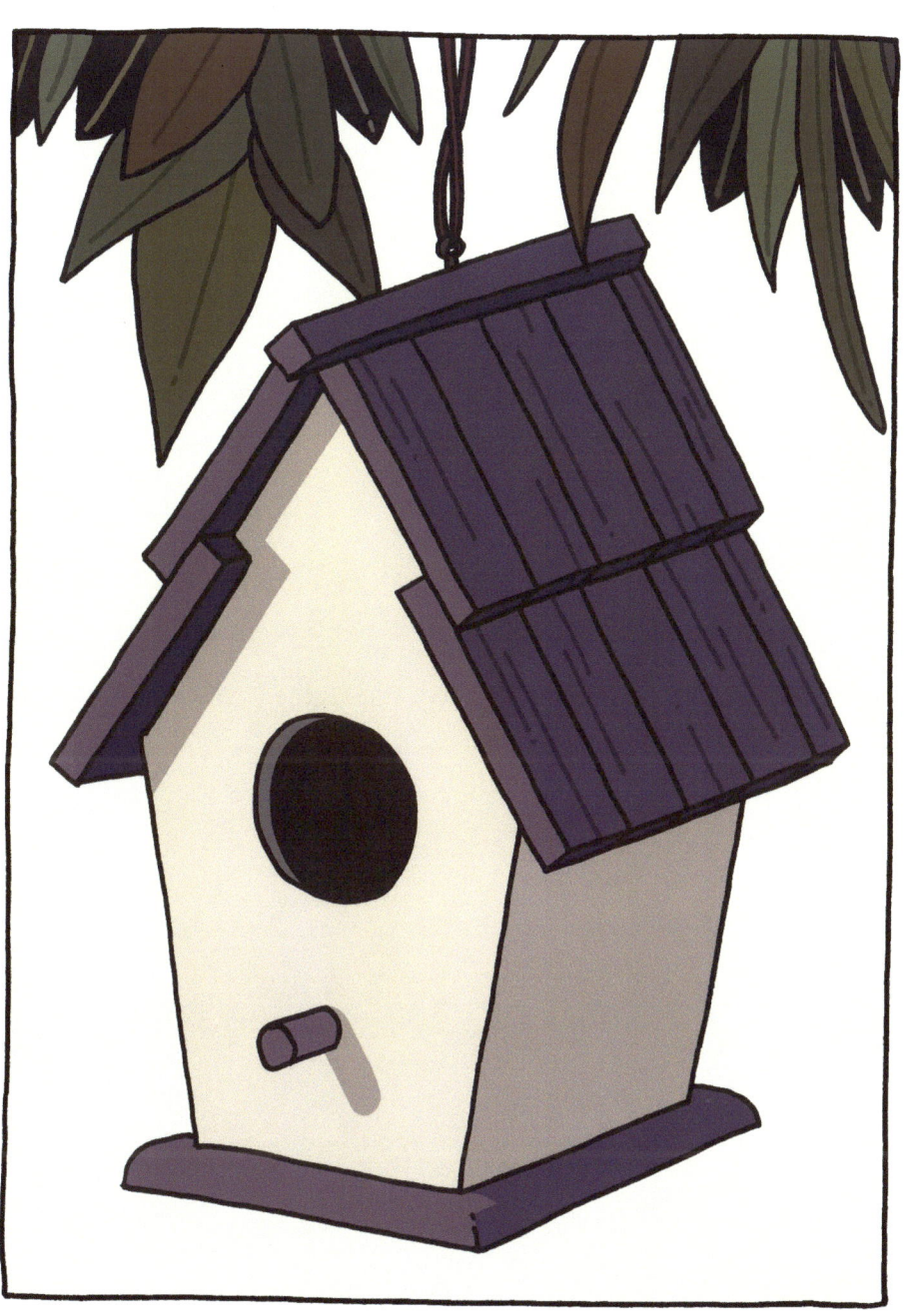

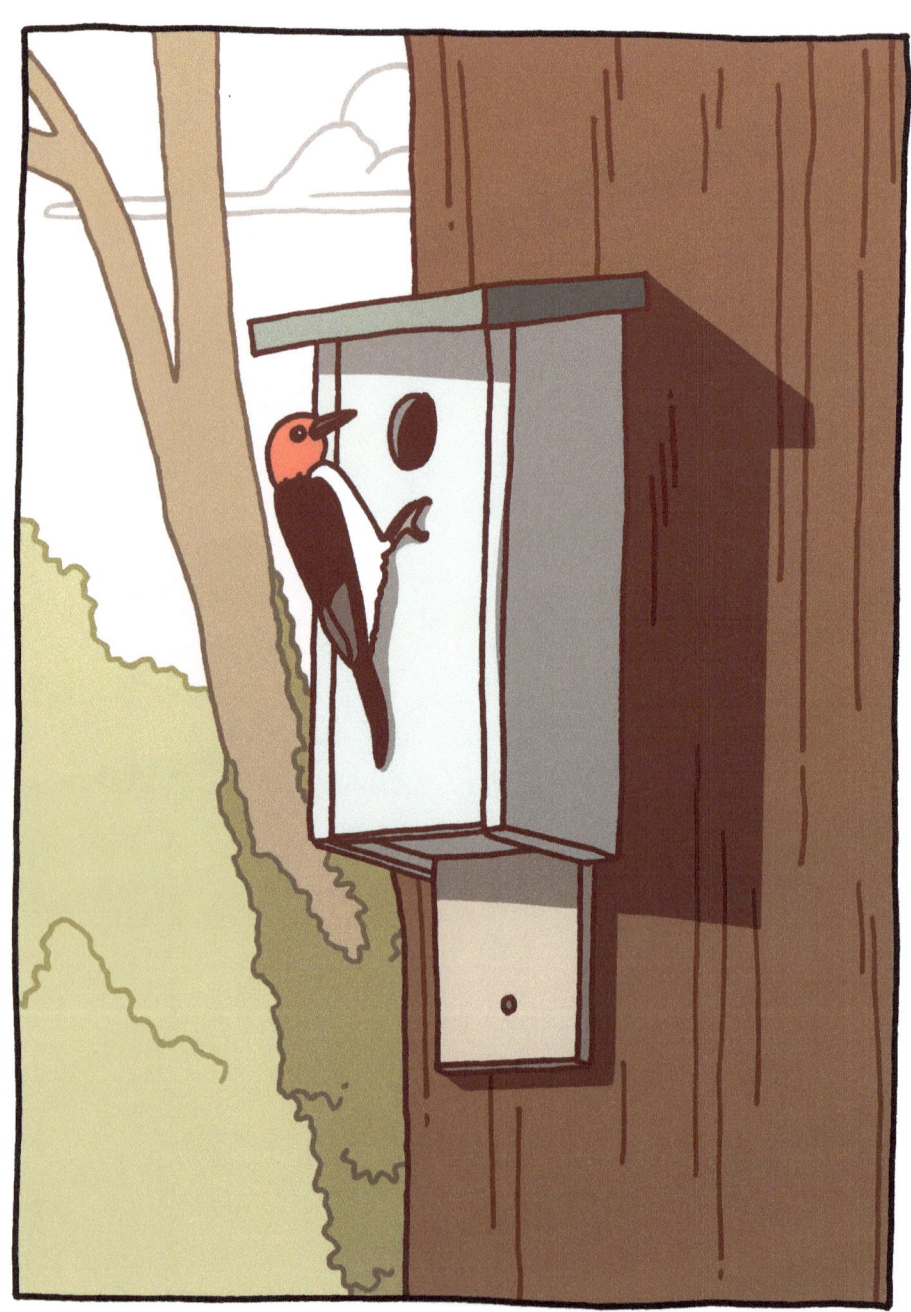

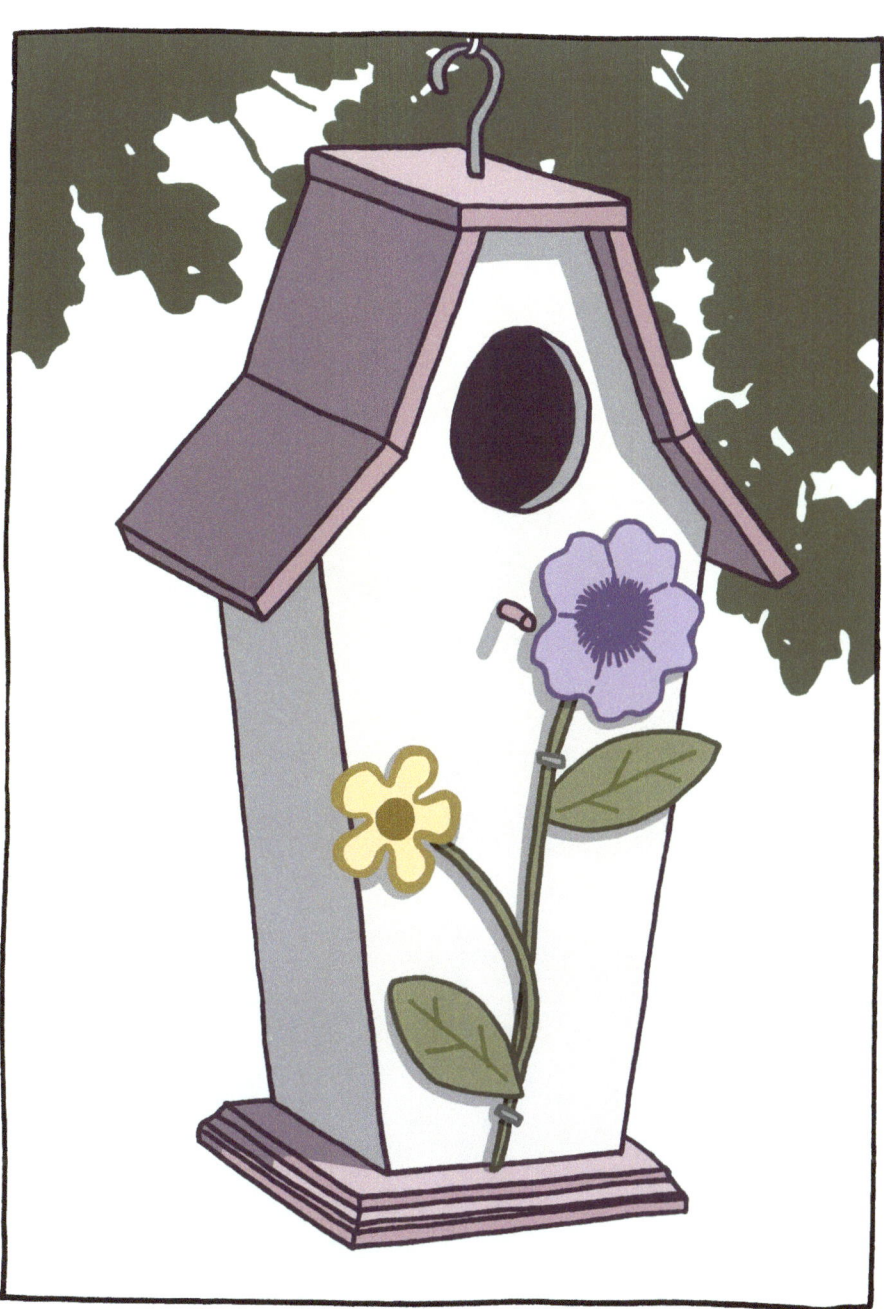

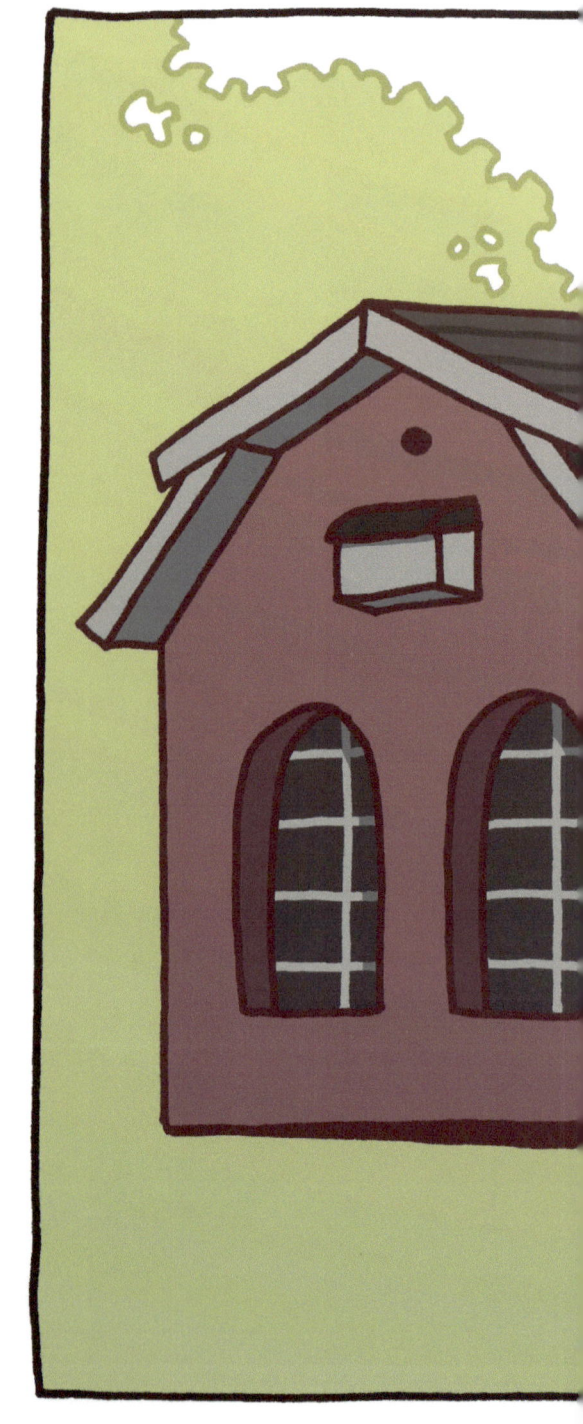

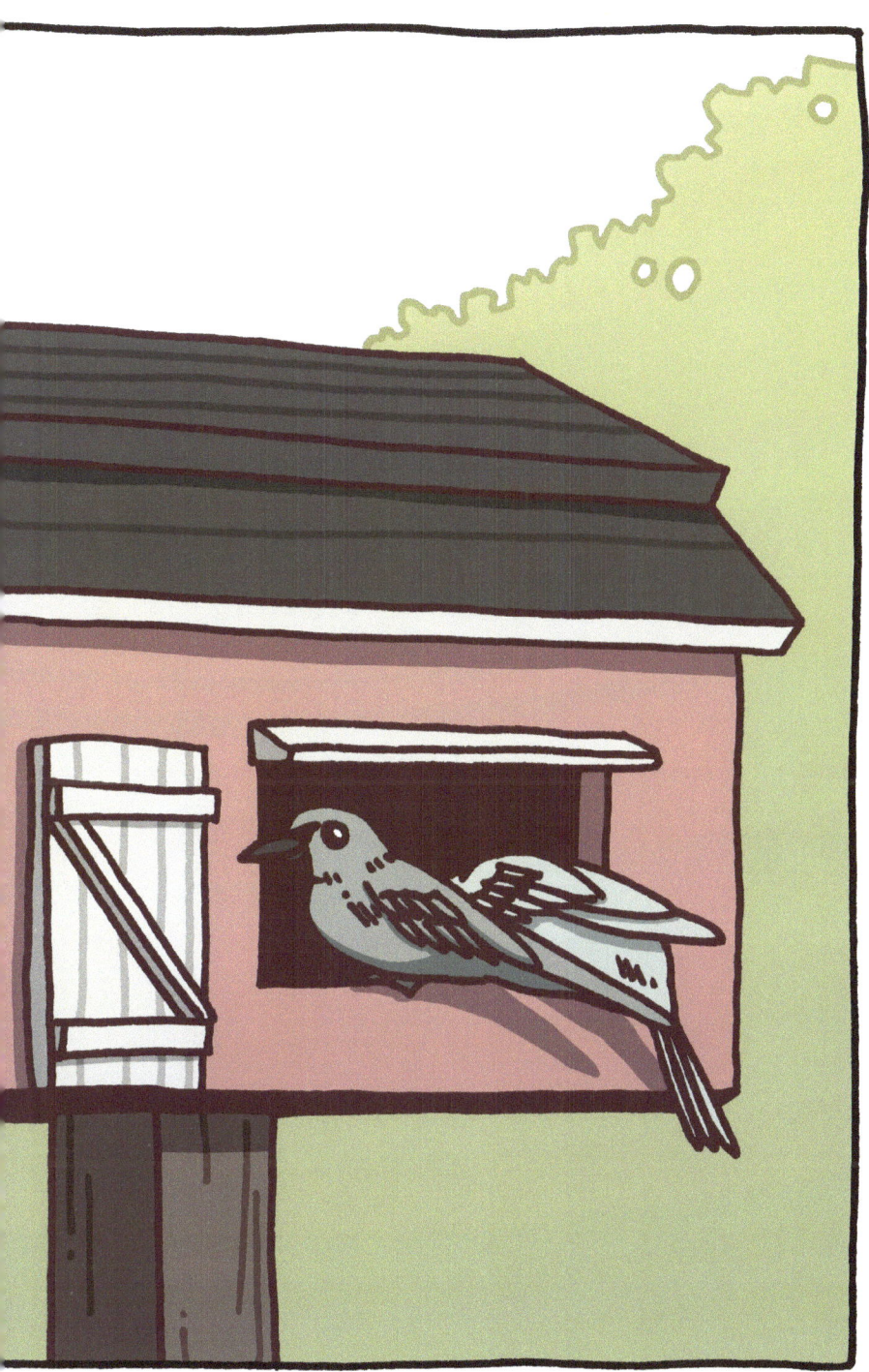

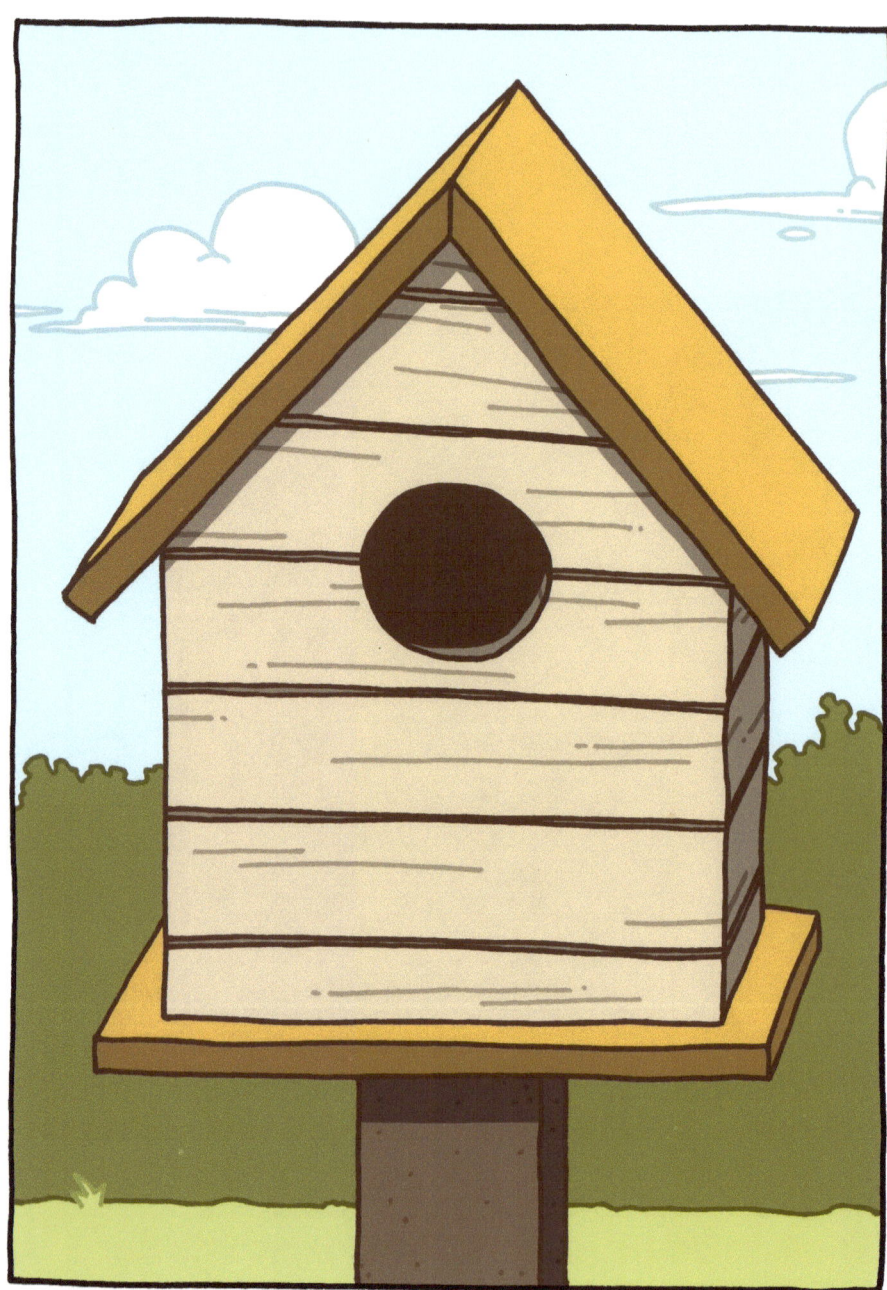

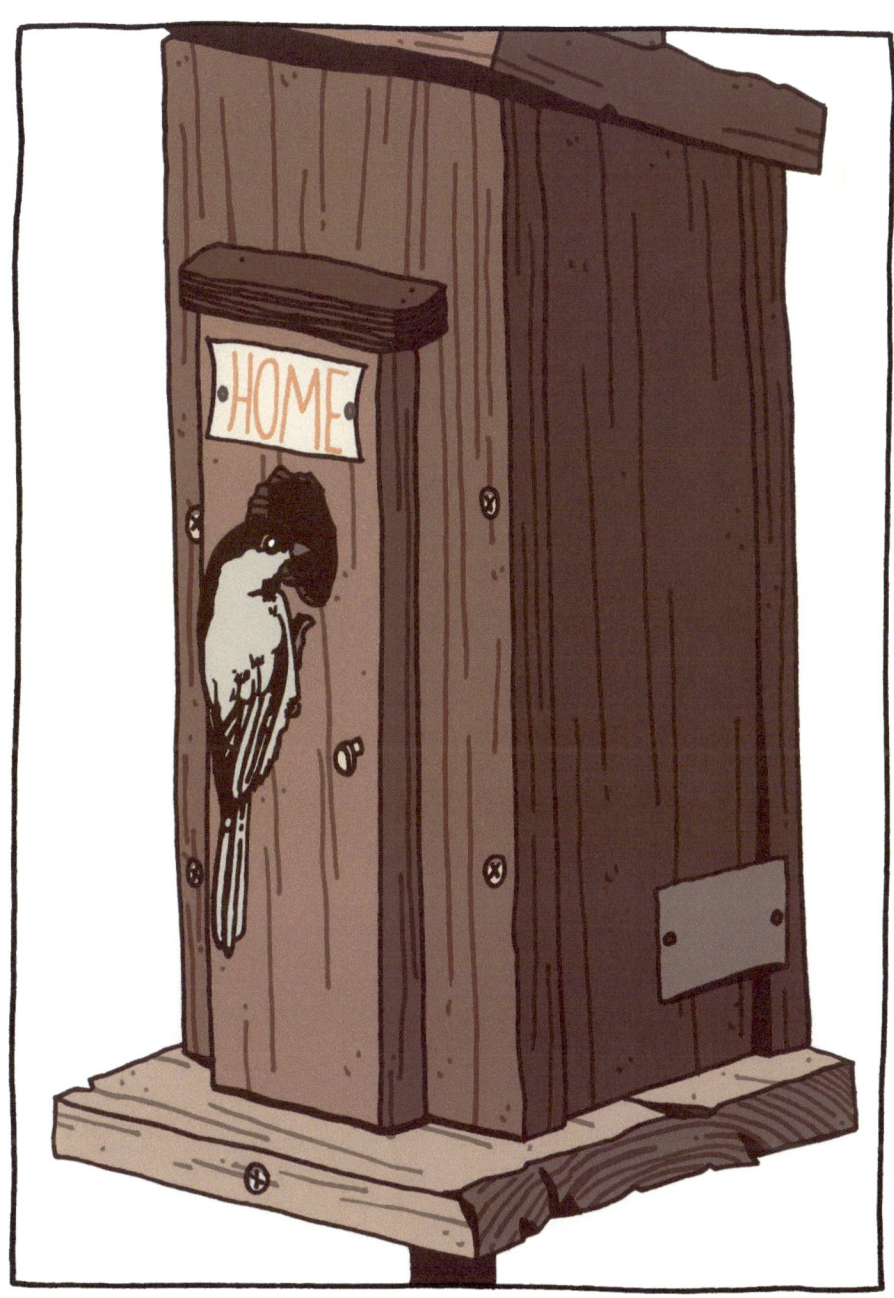

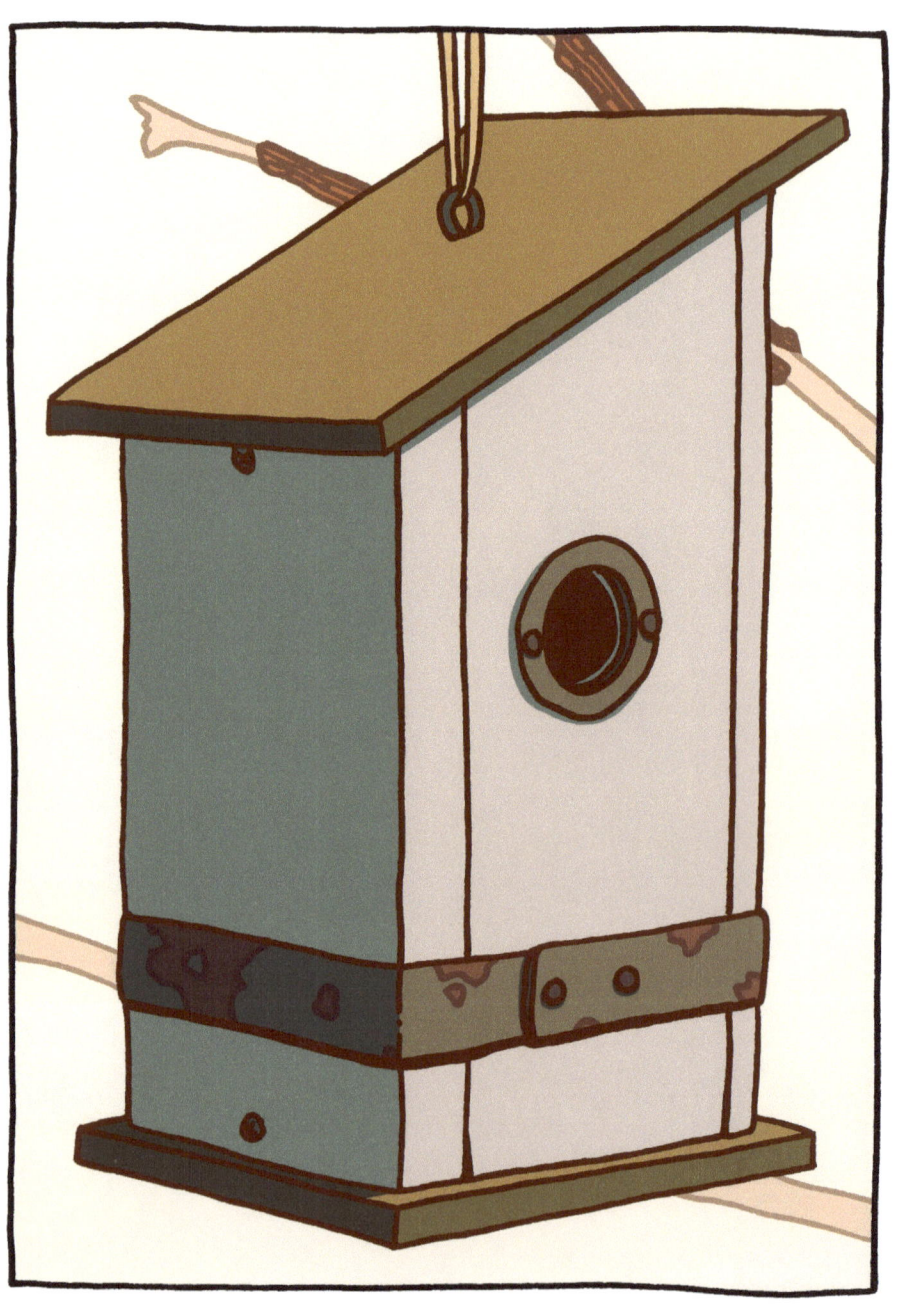

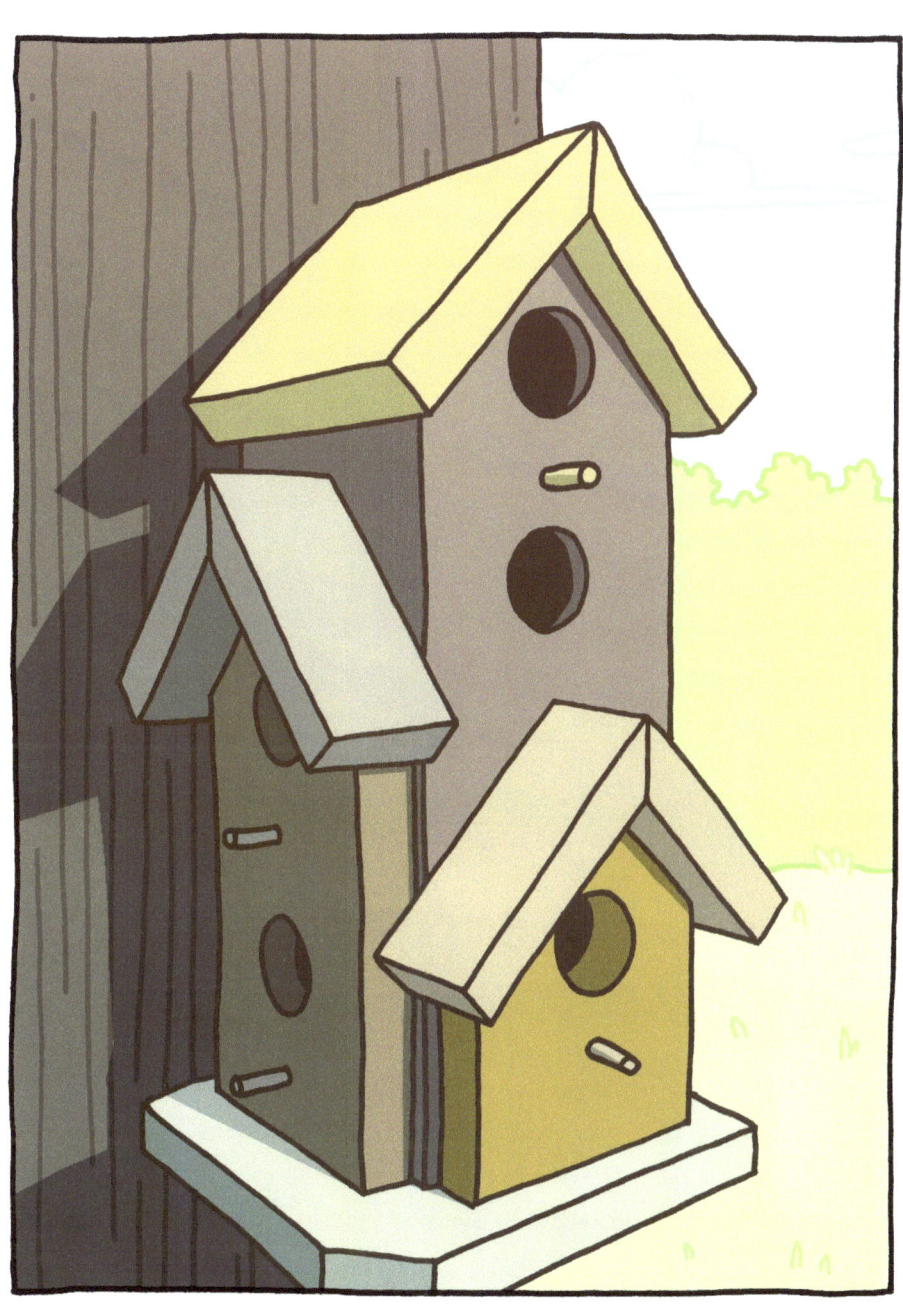

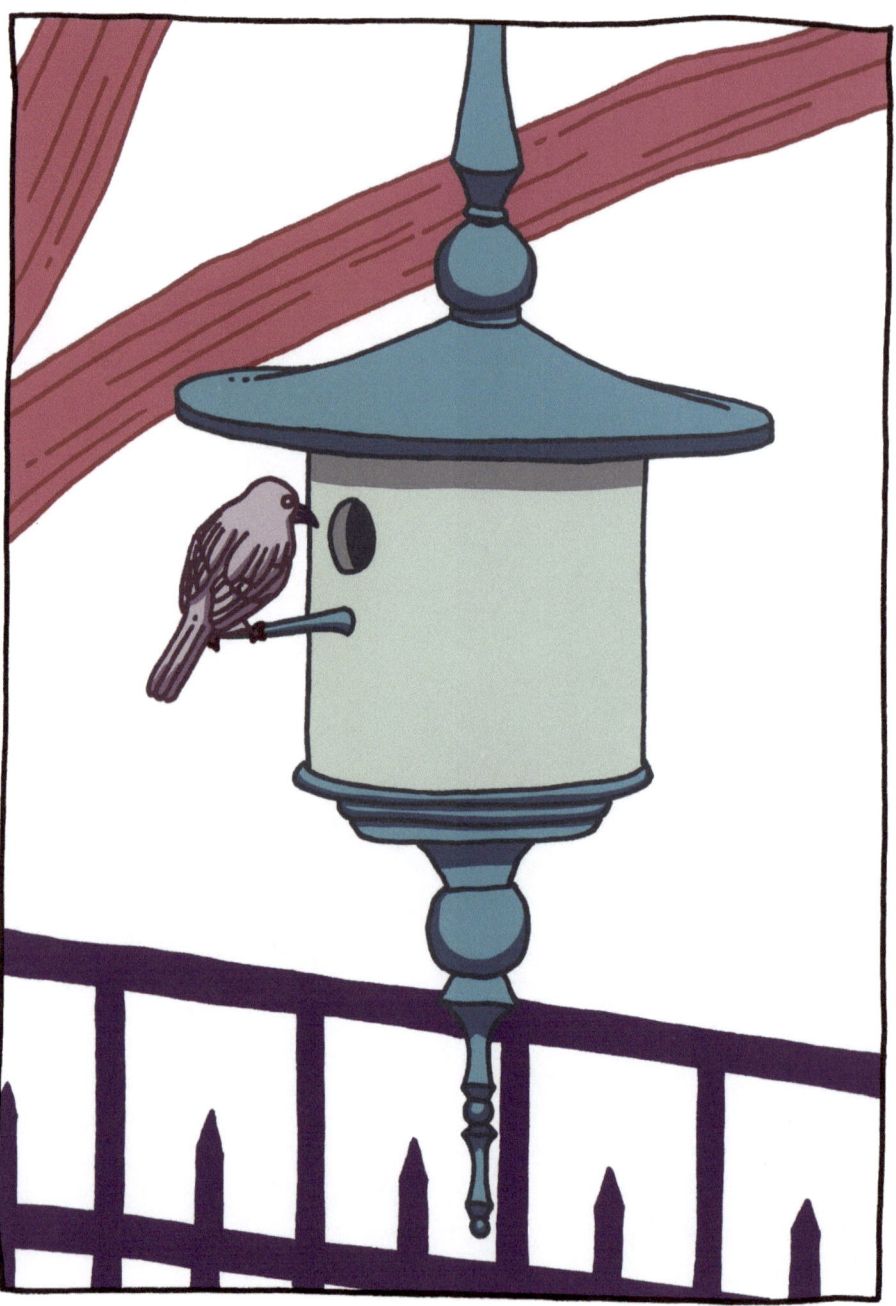

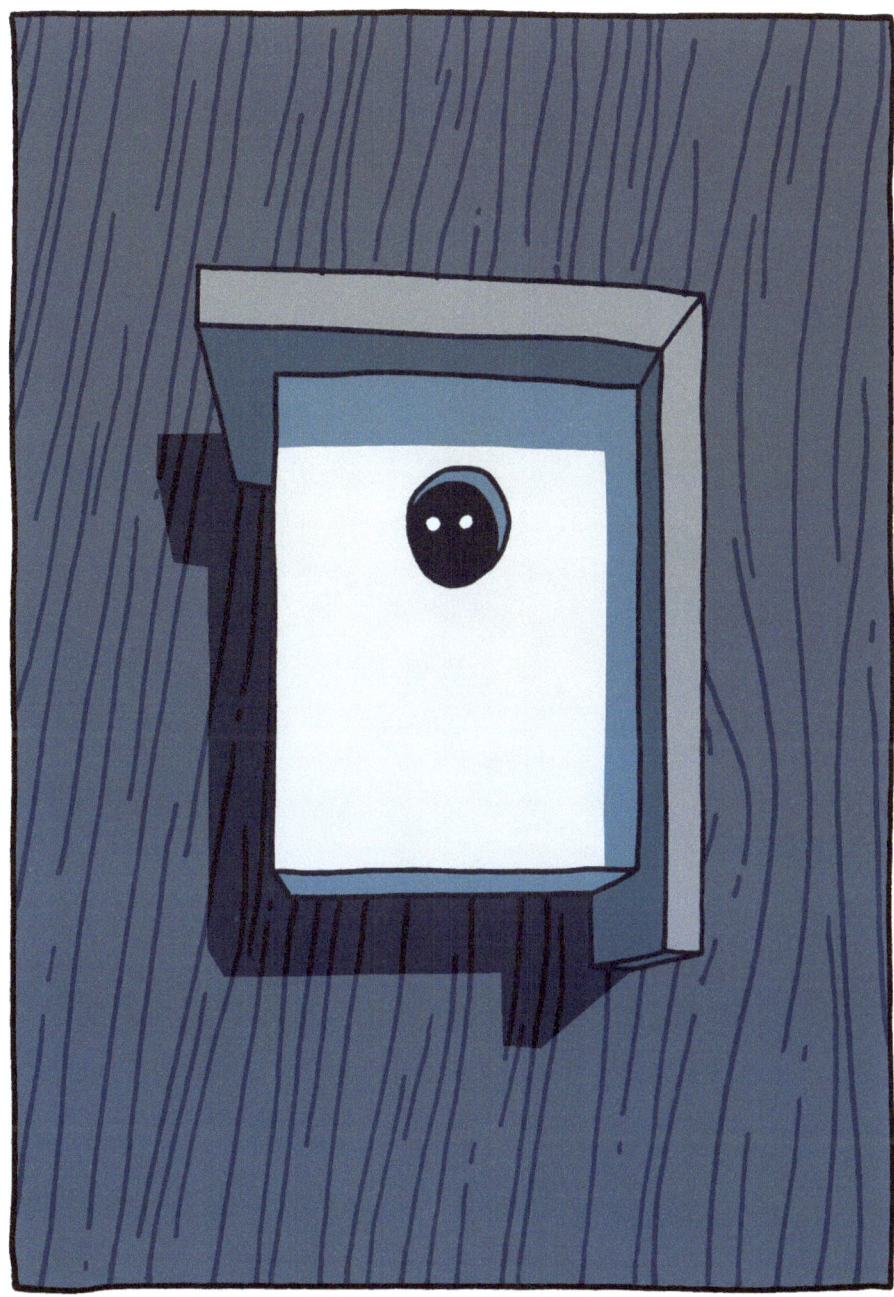

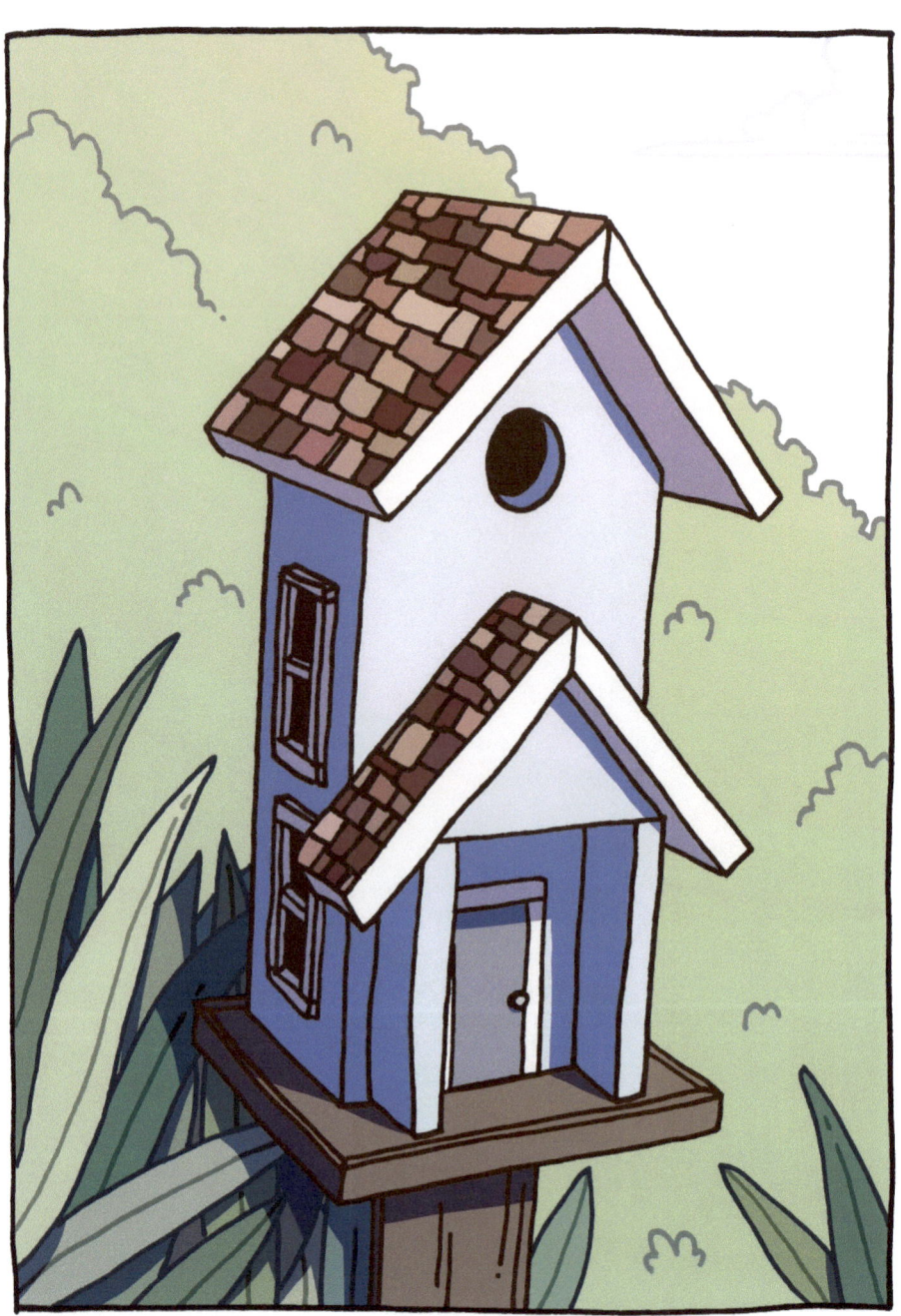

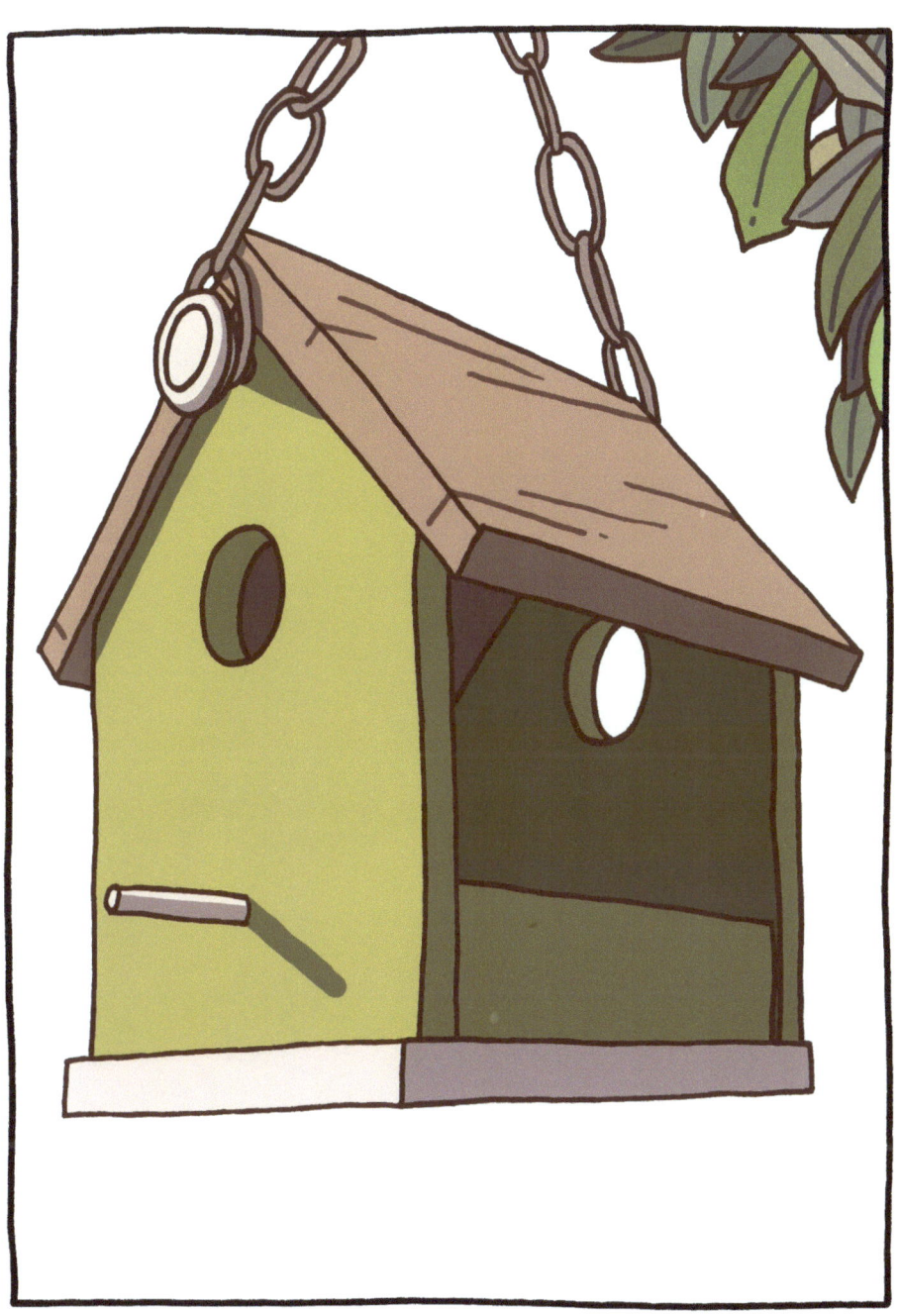

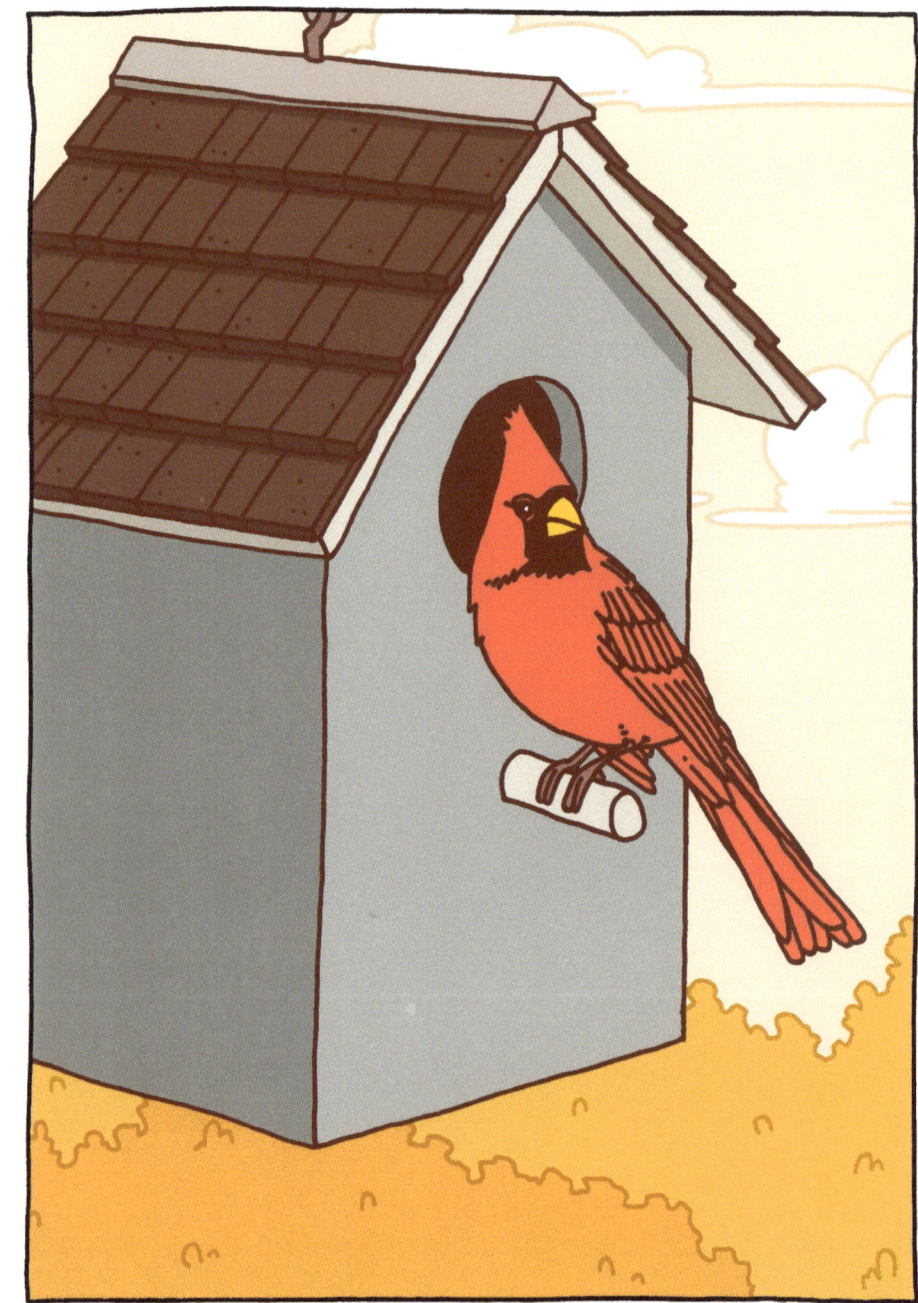

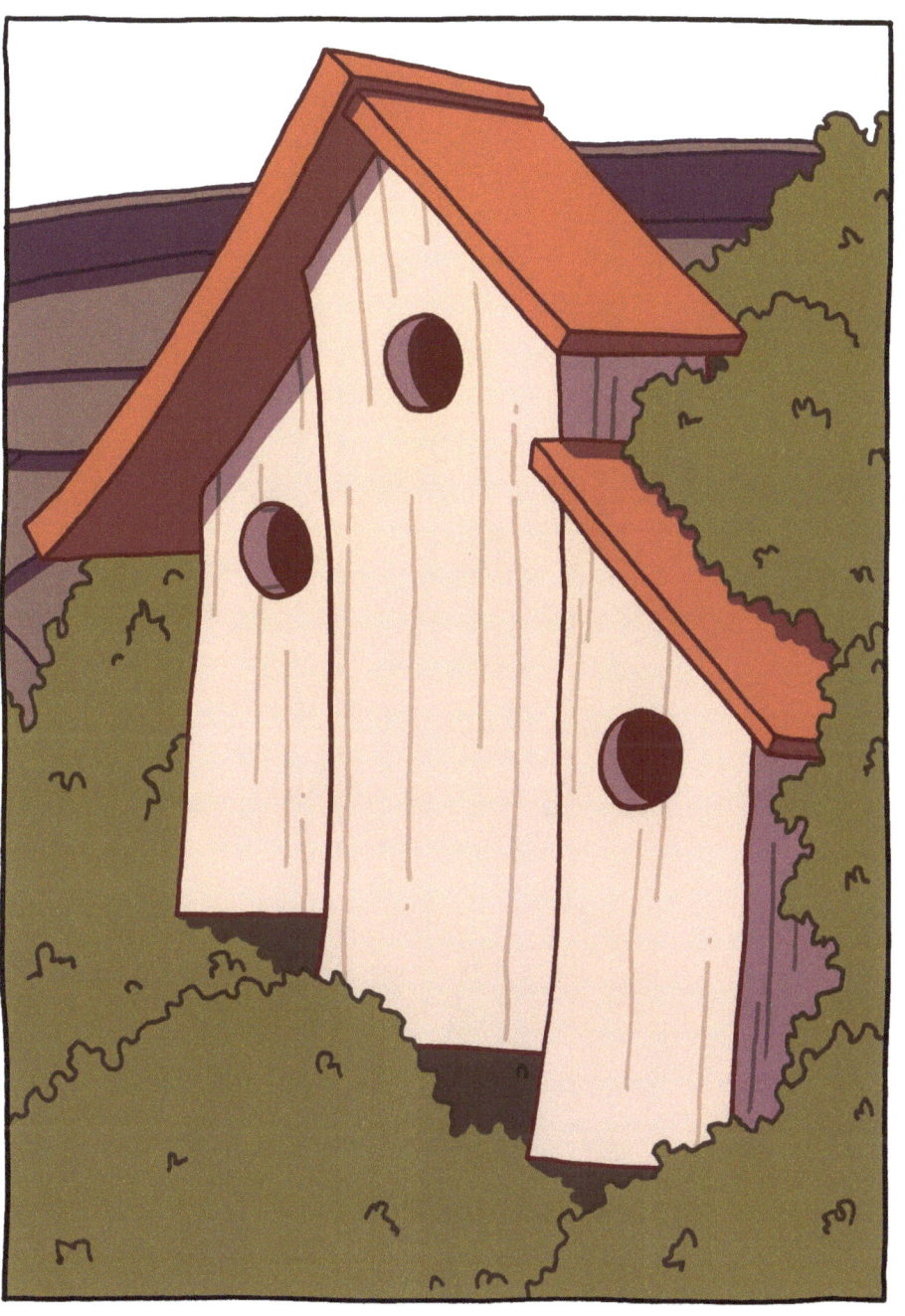

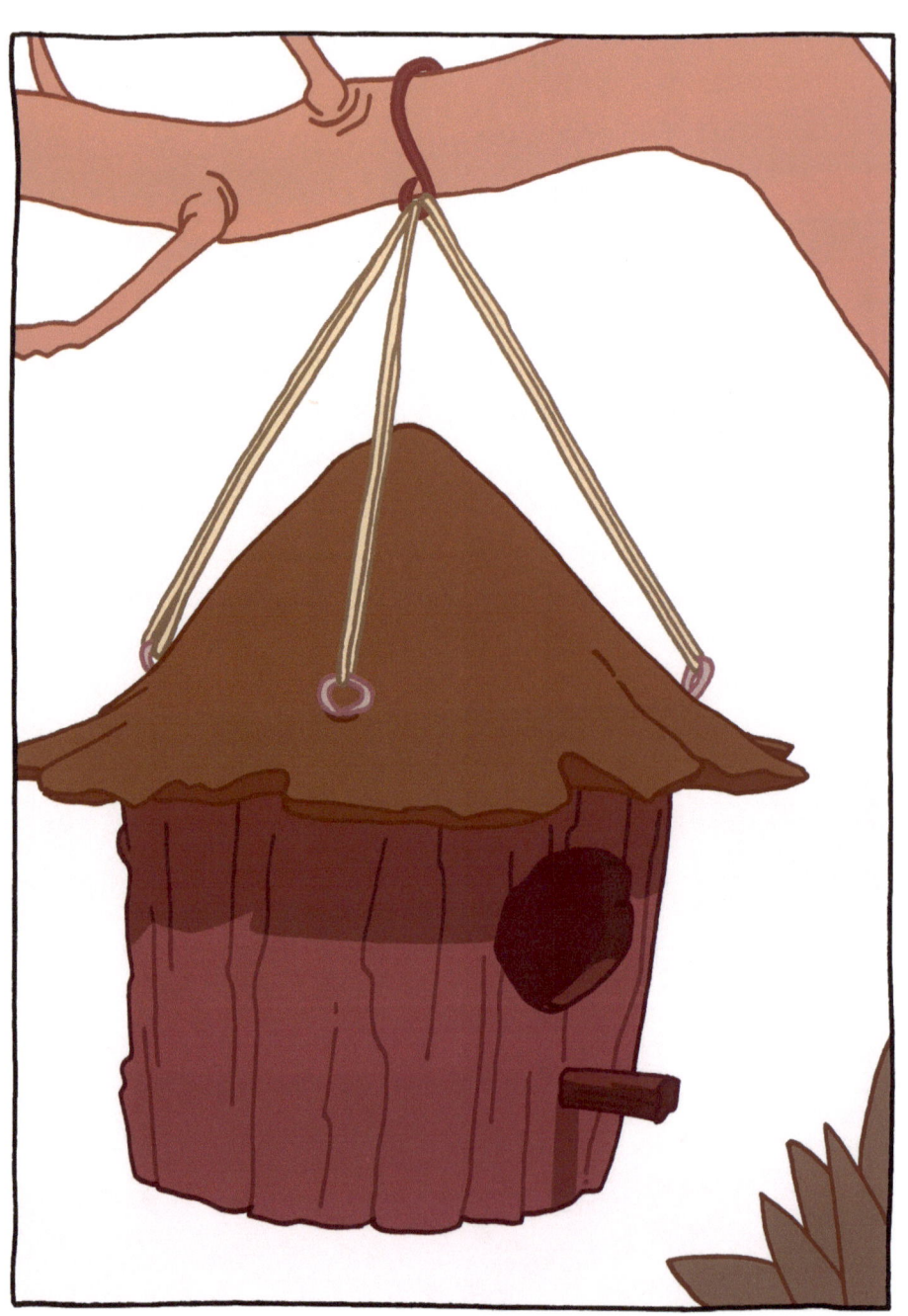

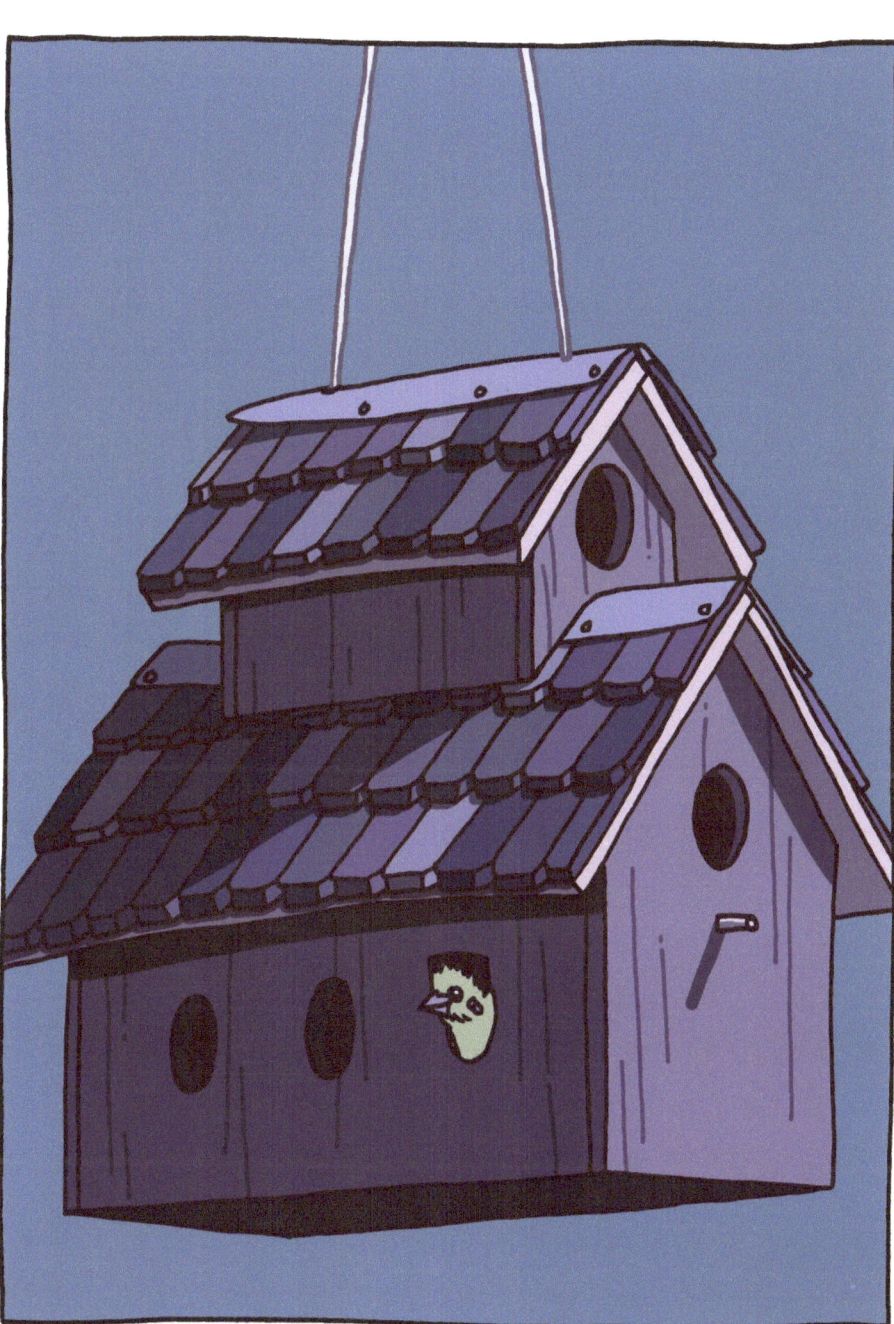

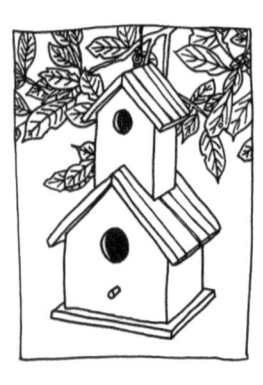
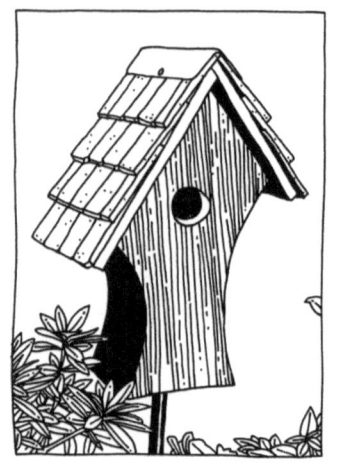
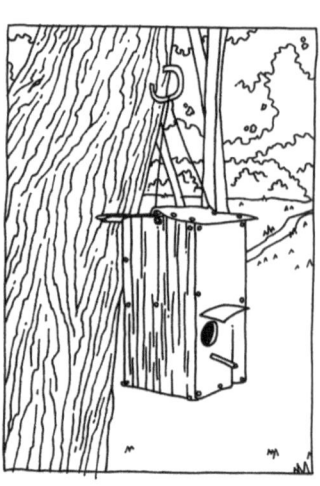
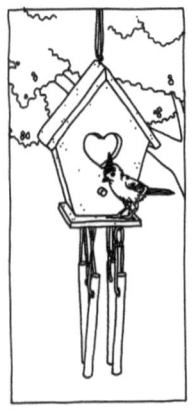
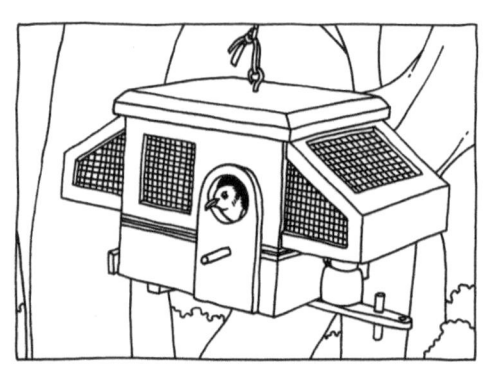
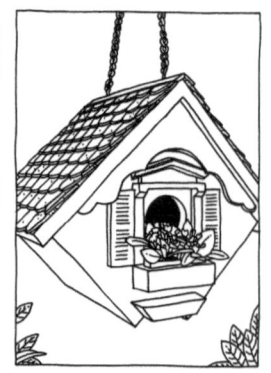
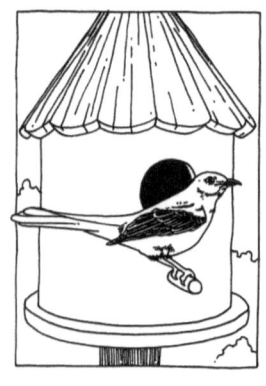
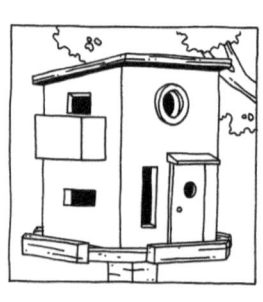
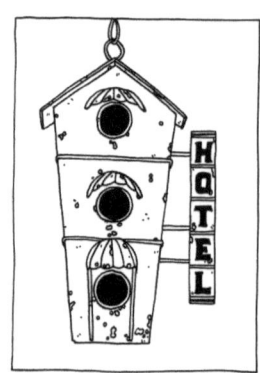

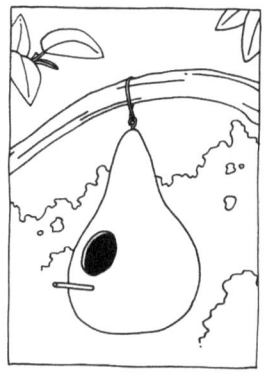
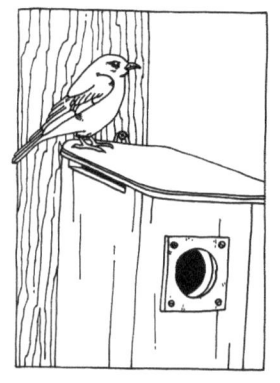
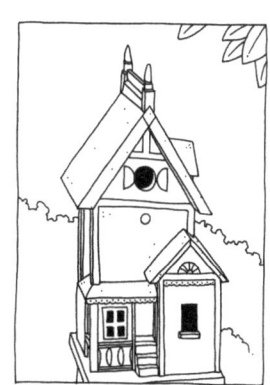
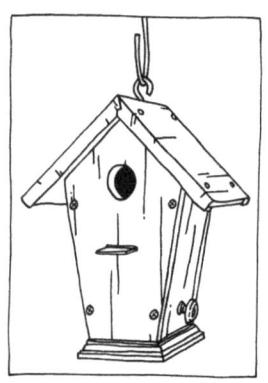
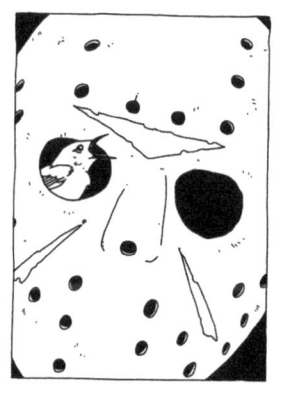
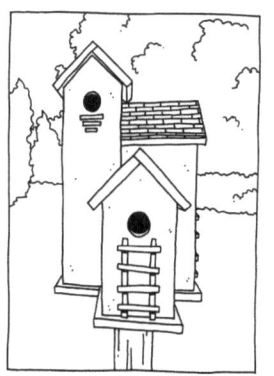
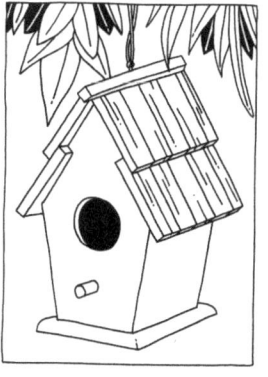
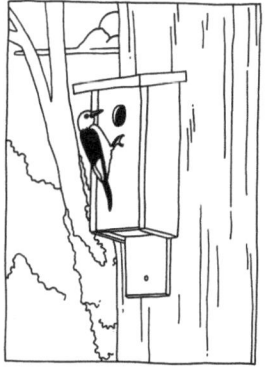
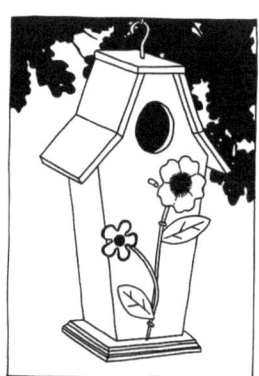

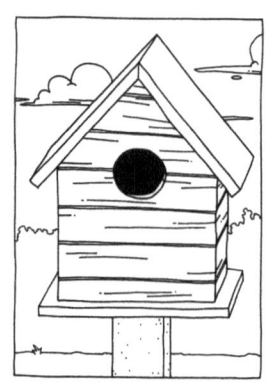
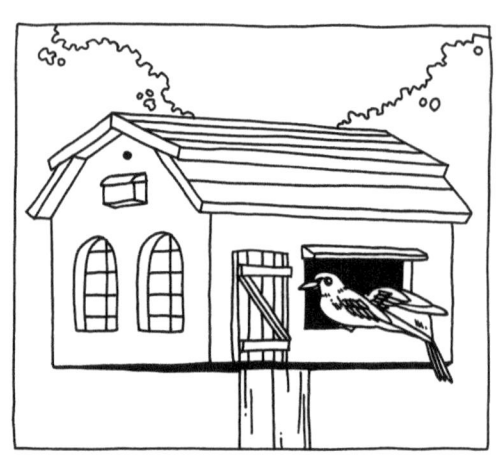
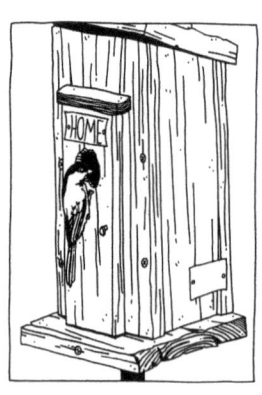
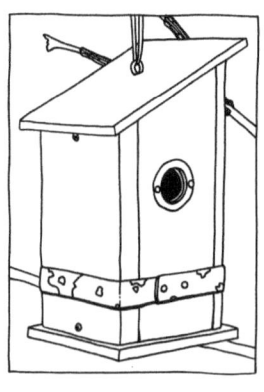
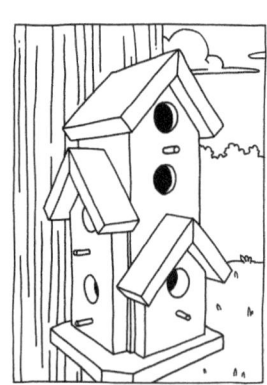
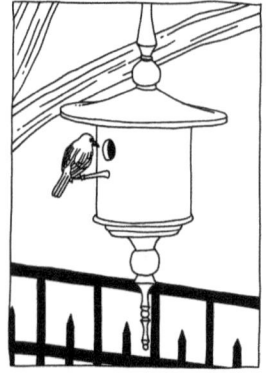
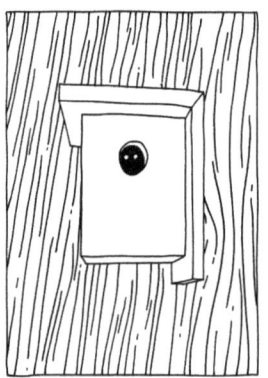
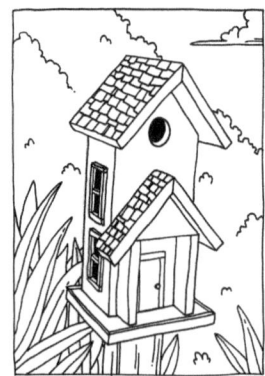

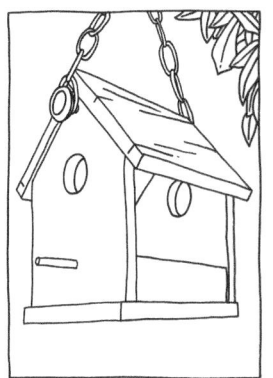
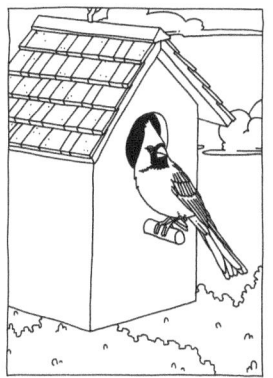
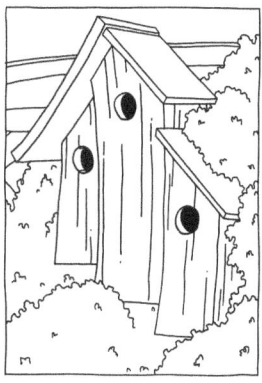
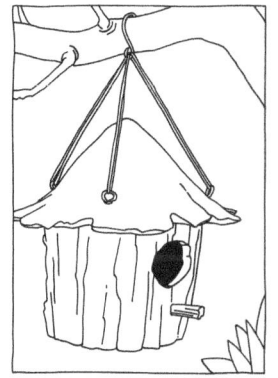
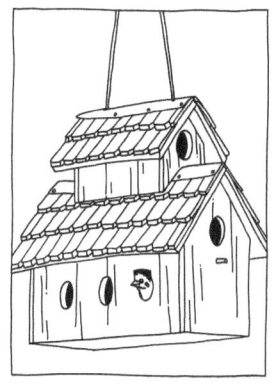

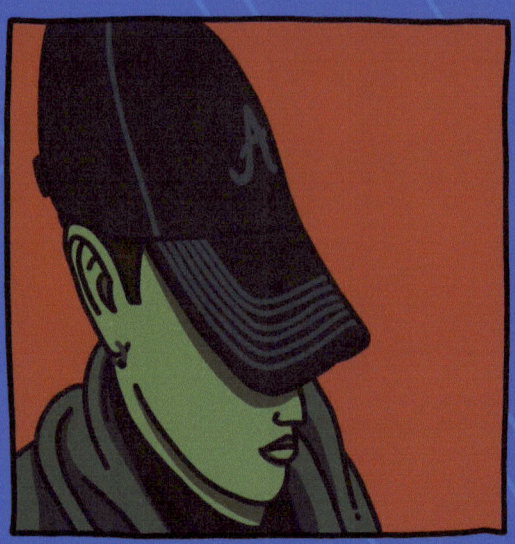

Nathan Lumm has spent the last 20+ years working in both the comic book and advertising industries, but has recently gone out on his own, into the world of freelance illustration. He currently resides in Texas, with his lovely wife and their adorable bunny.

More of his work can be found at:
instagram.com/nathan_lumm
youtube.com/user/lummage

www.ingramcontent.com/pod-product-compliance
Lightning Source LLC
Chambersburg PA
CBHW040336220526
45473CB00009B/2709